A West Yorkshire Playhouse
and Citizens Theatre co-production

Doctor Faustus

By Christopher Marlowe
and Colin Teevan

INTRODUCTION

Doctor Faustus is one of the great works of the classical canon, which many people know but not so many people have read or seen. West Yorkshire Playhouse and Citizens Theatre, Glasgow have always taken pride in being places where people can see great classical drama, not as museum pieces, but as vital and engaging works of drama, responsive to their time and place.

In producing any play, classical or contemporary, you ask the same question: why do this play now? What is it saying, what is it doing for this audience? Marlowe's Doctor Faustus has clear contemporary resonances, obsession with material possession, celebrity, a 'magical' transformation from nothing to fame and fortune. The thinking behind writing two new acts which are inspired by but not necessarily based on the original was first to replace two acts of dubious origin and even more dubious quality and then to explore more fully who is John Faustus in the modern world. The original play (not necessarily all Marlowe's own work) sits somewhere between the medieval mystery play and the new emergent Renaissance drama. Colin Teevan's new acts hold hands with Marlowe's beginning and end; retaining the sense of morality tale while bridging the gap with a clearer sense of narrative and character development. Bringing together the classic and contemporary; old and new language; and worlds abutting each other, feels entirely true to the adventurous, questing spirit of Marlowe and the original play.

Any production is the result of the particular combination of people who have created it, and indeed the people who see it. This is not the definitive version of Doctor Faustus, as no great piece of theatre can ever be wholly 'defined'. It is rather our version of Marlowe's great play re-imagined for here and now, made for and shared with you.

James Brining, Artistic Director, West Yorkshire Playhouse
Dominic Hill, Artistic Director, Citizens Theatre

CAST
(in alphabetical order)

Wagner – **Leah Brotherhead**
Duchess Robyn – **Esther Ruth Elliott**
Devil, Scholar, Party Attendee – **Alasdair Hankinson**
Cornelius – **Christopher Keegan**
Valdes – **John Kielty**
Lucifer, Pope, Bruno, President – **Gary Lilburn**
Mephistopheles – **Siobhan Redmond**
Good Angel – **Ann Louise Ross**
Doctor Faustus – **Kevin Trainor**
Bad Angel – **Oliver Wilson**

All other parts to be played by members of the company

Director – **Dominic Hill**
Designer – **Colin Richmond**
Lighting Designer – **Tim Mitchell**
Composer and Sound Designer – **Dan Jones**
Illusion Designers – **James Freedman** and **Ben Hart**
Movement Director – **Kally Lloyd-Jones**
Casting Director – **Camilla Evans**
Assistant Director – **Andrew Whyment** (Birkbeck Trainee)
Stage Managers – **Julie Issott** and **Natalia Cortes**
Deputy Stage Manager – **Cathy O'Neill**
Assistant Stage Managers – **Barry Forde** and **Rosanna Simpson**

Community Cast

Playing Young Faustus:	**Playing Young Faustus:**
Bobby Cook and George Rice	Finlay Jamieson and Adam Flynn

West Yorkshire Playhouse	**Citizens Theatre**
Nicoletta Baranelli	Robyn Ferguson
Peter Bartram	Beag Horn
Rudi Edwards	Jasmine Main
Beth Knight	Eirinn Mallon
Thea Mudhar	David McCaig
Amy Oddy	Rachel McGowan
Jacob Phillips	Jack Mullen
William Pugh	
Anne Reynold	
Liam Robbins	

THERE WILL BE ONE INTERVAL OF TWENTY MINUTES

The first performance of this production was
Saturday 23 February 2013 in the Quarry Theatre,
West Yorkshire Playhouse.

Performances at West Yorkshire Playhouse
23 February – 16 March, 2013

Performances at Citizens Theatre
5 – 27 April, 2013

Production Thanks:
Jonny Boutwood – Casting Assistant
Derren Brown – Voice Over

BSL Interpreted Performance:
Thursday 7 March 7.30 p.m. at West Yorkshire Playhouse
Alan Haythornwaite

Thursday 18 April at Citizens Theatre

Audio Described Performances:
Friday 8 March 7.30 p.m. and Thursday 14 March 1.30 p.m.
Anne Muers and Lynn Thornton
at West Yorkshire Playhouse

Thursday 11 April at Citizens Theatre

Captioned Performance:
Friday 15 March 7.30 p.m. at West Yorkshire Playhouse
Alina Secăra

Thursday 25 April at Citizens Theatre

CAST

LEAH BROTHERHEAD
Theatre credits include: **People Like Us** (The Pleasance); **DNA** (UK Tour); **The Kitchen Sink** (Bush Theatre); **Euphoria** (Fruit); **Sum Zero** (Lyric Hammersmith); **Product Placement** (Watford Palace); **Time Warner Ignite 2&4** (Waterloo East); **The 24 Hour Plays: Old Vic New Voices** (Old Vic); **The House of Bernarda Alba** (Tristan Bates); **Eye/Balls** and **Victory Street** (Soho).

Film and television credits include: **Vera, Doctors** and **Jess/Jim.**

Leah is a Carleton Hobbs award winner and has recorded various radio dramas with the BBC including **The Archers, I,Claudius, The Big Sleep, Danton's Death, The Far Pavillions** and **Showboat.**

ESTHER RUTH ELLIOTT
Esther trained at Bristol Old Vic Theatre School.

Theatre credits include: **Top Girls** (Out Of Joint/No 1 Tour); **The New World Order** (Barbican/Hydrocracker); **The Importance of Being Earnest** (New Wolsley, Ipswich); **Oliver Twist** (Bolton Octagon Theatre); **Measure for Measure, The Taming of the Shrew** and **Cymbeline** (Royal Shakespeare Company); **The Three Sisters, Twelfth Night, Pericles** and **The Winter's Tale** (Shakespeare at the Tobacco Factory); **Reading Hebron, Leaving** and **Once We Were Mothers** (Orange Tree, Richmond); **Cariad** (Theatr Clwyd); **The Erpingham Camp** (Hydrocracker, Brighton Festival) and **Intimate Exchanges** (Theatre Royal, Bury St Edmunds).

Television credits include: **Emmerdale, Heartbeat, Casualty** and various plays for Radio 4.

ALASDAIR HANKINSON

Alasdair graduated from the Royal Conservatoire of Scotland in July 2012.

His professional credits include: **Sleeping Beauty** (Citizens Theatre); **#neednothing** (Arches Live!); **The History Boys** (Greenwich Theatre); **Kasimir and Karoline** (National Theatre of Scotland Rehearsal Reading) and **The Legend of Captain Crow's Teeth** (Unicorn Theatre, London).

Whilst training, Alasdair was the recipient of a Laurence Olivier Bursary and is currently one of the two Citizens Theatre Actor Interns.

CHRISTOPHER KEEGAN

Christopher trained at the Drama Centre London, graduating in 2009. He was born in Bury St Edmunds, Suffolk and grew up in Hebden Bridge, West Yorkshire. Whilst there he joined the Calderdale Theatre School in nearby Halifax and won the NODA Award for Best Leading Male in a Junior Production for his portrayal of Henry Higgins in **My Fair Lady**.

Theatre credits include: **The History Boys** (UK tour); **The Madness of George III** (Theatre Royal, Bath); **The Taming of the Shrew** (Shakespeare's Globe Theatre); **Sense** (Company of Angels/Southwark Playhouse); **As You Like It**, **The Changeling**, **The Government Inspector**, **You Can't Take It With You**, **Awake and Sing**, **Emilia Galotti**, **Three Sisters** and **Pygmalion** (Drama Centre, London).

Television credits include: **Hustle** and **Doctors**.

JOHN KIELTY

John is an actor, a writer and a musician.

Recent theatre credits include: **The Bible: Abridged** (Reduced Shakespeare Company); **Roman Bridge, Mary Queen of Scots Got Her Head Chopped Off, Our Teachers a Troll** (National Theatre of Scotland); **Sleeping Beauty** (Citizens Theatre); **The Cone Gatherers** (His Majesty's Theatre, Aberdeen); **The 27 Club** (Forever 27 Productions); **Whatever Gets You Through The Night** (The Arches); **Confessions of a Justified Sinner** and **The Cherry Orchard** (Royal Lyceum, Edinburgh).

Theatre scores include: **The Cone Gatherers** (His Majesty's Theatre, Aberdeen); **Why Do You Stand There in the Rain?** (Pepperdine University Malibu: Winner Fringe First 2012); **Medea's Children** (Ungla Klara/Lung Has); **Educating Agnes** (Theatre Babel) and **Merlin the Magnificent** (Royal Lyceum, Edinburgh).

He has written many new musicals including: **The 27 Club,** (Forever 27 Productions); **Active Virgin** (RCS); **Wasted Love** (RCS – Winner Best Lyrics MTM 2011); **The Murder of Geoffrey Robbins** (Òran Mór); **Greyfriar's Twisted Tales** (Bridewell Theatre Company – Winner Spirit of Fringe 2008); **Mercy Madonna of Malawi** (World Stage Productions – Winner Spirit of Fringe 2009) and **Sundowe** (Eden Court – Winner Cameron Mackintosh's 'Quest for a New Musical').

John also recently collaborated on Cora Bissett's new musical **Glasgow Girls** (National Theatre of Scotland).

GARY LILBURN

Theatre credits include: **The Kingdom** (Soho Theatre); **Buried Child** (Leicester Curve); **16 Possible Glimpses** (Dublin Abbey Theatre); **Loot** (Hull Truck); **The Hostage** (Southwark Playhouse); **Calendar Girls** (West End and tour); **The Man Who Had All The Luck** (Donmar Warehouse); **Dancing at Lughnasa** (Manchester Library); **The Quare Fellow** (Tricycle and tour); **Death of a Salesman** (Leicester Haymarket); **Hen House** (Arcola); **The Golden Ass, A Midsummer Night's Dream** (Globe); **Buried Alive** (Hampstead); **The Weir** (Royal Court); **Angels and Saints** (Soho); **Desire under the Elms** (Shared Experience); **Waiting for Godot, Blood Knot** (New Victoria, Stoke); **One Flew Over The Cuckoo's Nest** (West End) and **Beggar's Opera** (Druid).

Television credits include: **Mrs Brown's Boys, Doctors, Pete Versus Life, I Shouldn't Be Alive, Casualty, Whistleblower, Single Handed, Perfect Day: The Funeral, Pulling, Sea of Souls, Grease Monkeys, The Bill, 55 Degrees North, EastEnders, Dalziel & Pascoe, My Family, McReady & Daughters, Fair City.**

Film credits include: **Philomena, Eden, Garage, Veronica Guerin** and **4 Conversations About Love.**

SIOBHAN REDMOND

Theatre credits include: **King John, Richard III, Spanish Tragedy, Twelfth Night, Much Ado About Nothing** (Royal Shakespeare Company); **Dunsinane** (National Theatre of Scotland/Royal Shakespeare Company); **Celebrity Autobiography** (Glasgow Comedy Festival); **The Secret Garden** (Festival Theatre, Edinburgh); **A Midsummer Night's Dream** (Shakespeare's Globe); **House of Bernarda Alba, Mary Stuart** (National Theatre of Scotland); **Dido – Queen of Carthage** (National Theatre); **U.S. and Them** (Hampstead Theatre); **The Prime of Miss Jean Brodie** (Royal Lyceum, Edinburgh); **An Experienced Woman Gives Advice** (Manchester Royal Exchange); **The Trick is to Keep Breathing** (Tron Theatre); **A Midsummer Night's Dream** and **King Lear** (Renaissance Theatre Company).

Television credits include: **Bob Servant, Case Histories II, The Town, Benidorm, Taggart, Midway, Boy Meets Girl, The Bill, Lift, The Catherine Tate Show, The Smoking Room, Sea of Souls, In the Red, Wokenwell, Deacon Brodie, Nervous Energy, Relative Stranger, About Last Night, The High Life, Between the Lines.**

ANN LOUISE ROSS

Ann Louise Ross has been a member of Dundee Rep ensemble for the past 13 years. She has won two TMA Awards for Best Supporting Actress for **The Winter's Tale** and **Sunshine on Leith** and a 2012 CATS Award for Best Actress in **Further Than the Furthest Thing**.

Theatre credits include: **Further than the Furthest Thing, Sunshine on Leith, The Winter's Tale, Gypsy, Peer Gynt, Ubu the King, Steel Magnolias, Sweeney Todd, Mother Courage, Romeo and Juliet, If Destroyed True** (Dundee Rep); **Guid Sisters** (National Theatre of Scotland/Royal Lyceum, Edinburgh); **Mary Queen of Scotts Got Her Head Chopped Off** and **Age of Arousal** (Royal Lyceum, Edinburgh).

Television credits include: **Case Histories, Bob Servant Independent, Rebus: Let it Bleed, The Bill, The Key, Life Support, Looking After Jo Jo** and **Hamish Macbeth.**

Film credits include: **Split Second; Trainspotting; The Witch's Daughter** and **The Acid House Trilogy: Granton Star Cause.**

KEVIN TRAINOR
Theatre credits include: **Twelfth Night, Solstice, The Comedy of Errors, Eric La Rue** (Royal Shakespeare Company); **Playboy of the Western World, Six Degrees of Separation** (Old Vic); **Canary** (Liverpool Everyman/Hampstead); **Lost Monsters**; (Liverpool Everyman); **Bent** (West End); **Gladiator Games** (Stratford East); **Titanic** (MAC Belfast); **By Jeeves** (Landor); **Fishbowl** (Theatre 503).

Television credits include: **The Café** (series one and two); **John Adams; The Catherine Tate Show; Vera; Sherlock; Tripping Over; The Commander; Titanic: Birth of a Legend**.

Film credits include: **Hellboy; Make it New, John**.

OLIVER WILSON
Theatre credits includes: **Blue/Orange** (ATG, Theatre Royal Brighton/UK Tour); **Emperor and Galilean** (National Theatre); **Romeo and Juliet** (York Theatre Royal/Pilot Theatre and UK Tour); **Antony and Cleopatra** (Nuffield Theatre); **All's Well that Ends Well** (National Theatre/Olivier) **Pigeon Love** (The Space); **Much Ado About Nothing** (Derby Live); **This Child** (Pilot Theatre Company); **The Gala, World Poetry Day** Recital and Seven Ages of Poetry (Royal Shakespeare Company).

Film and television credits include: **Misfits, Hollyoaks, Casualty, Groove Town** and **Karmic Compensation**.

CREATIVES

DOMINIC HILL Director
Dominic Hill is Artistic Director of the Citizens Theatre in Glasgow and has directed **Sleeping Beauty**, **Krapp's Last Tape** and **Footfalls**, **King Lear** and **Betrayal** (winner of Best Director, 2012 Critics Awards for Theatre in Scotland) for the theatre. From 2008, he was Artistic Director of the Traverse Theatre in Edinburgh and prior to this he worked at Dundee Rep where he was first Associate Director and then, from 2003, Joint Artistic Director with James Brining. Highlights at the Traverse include: **The Last Witch** (a co-production with Edinburgh International Festival), **The Three Musketeers** and **the Princess of Spain** by Chris Hannan, **The Goat or Who is Sylvia?** by Edward Albee and **The Dark Things** by Ursula Rani Sarma. Directing highlights whilst at Dundee Rep include: **Happy Days**, **Hansel and Gretel**, **Midsummer Night's Dream**, **Monkey**, **The Talented Mr. Ripley**, **Ubu the King**, **The Graduate**, **Macbeth**, **Scenes from an Execution**, **Peter Pan**, **Twelfth Night**, **Dancing at Lughnasa**, **The Snow Queen**, **The Duchess of Mafia**, **The Winter's Tale** and a co-production of **Peer Gynt** (winner of four CATS Awards) with the National Theatre of Scotland. Other credits include **Falstaff** (Scottish Opera) and **The City Madam** (Royal Shakespeare Company). He has directed in theatres in London and throughout the UK.

COLIN TEEVAN Writer
Recent stage work includes: **The Kingdom** (Soho Theatre); **There Was A Man.**, **There Was No Man** (Tricycle Theatre, Bomb Season); **The Lion of Kabul** (Tricycle Theatre, Great Game Season); **How Many Miles to Basra?** (West Yorkshire Playhouse, winner of 2007 Clarion Award for Best New Play); **The Bee** and **The Diver** (Soho Theatre and NodaMap, Japan) both co-written with Hideki Noda. **Missing Persons, Four Tragedies, Roy Keane, Monkey!** (The Young Vic); **The Walls** (National Theatre) and **Alcmaeon in Corinth** (Live! Theatre).
Adaptations include: **Kafka's Monkey** (Young Vic); **Peer Gynt** (Dundee Rep and National Theatre Scotland, directed by Dominic Hill, winner of four CATS Awards); **Don Quixote** with Pablo Ley (West Yorkshire Playhouse) and **Svejk** (Gate Theatre/TFANA, NY).
Translations include: Euripides' **Bacchai** (National Theatre), Manfridi's **Cuckoos** (Gate/Barbican) both directed by Sir Peter Hall; **Marathon** by Edoardo Erba (Gate) and **Iph. . .** after Euripides (Lyric, Belfast).
Television includes: **Single Handed** for RTE and ITV, **Vera** for ITV. Colin has written over 20 plays for BBC Radio. He is currently senior lecturer in Creative Writing at Birkbeck College, University of London where he founded and convenes the BA in Creative Writing. All his work is published by Oberon Books.

COLIN RICHMOND Designer
Colin trained at the Royal Welsh
College of Music and Drama. First
Class BA Hons.
Lord Williams Design Award 2002
and 2003.
Linbury Prize Finalist.
Colin has designed for many theatres
throughout the UK, and in London.
A selection of design credits include:
Entertaining Mr Sloane, **Bad Girls
– The Musical**, **Breakfast With
Mugabe** (RSC) (all West End); **The
Cherry Orchard**, **A Christmas Carol**,
(Birmingham Rep Theatre); **Annie,
Bad Girls – The Musical**, **Animal
Farm**, **Billy Liar**, **A Christmas Carol**
(West Yorkshire Playhouse); **L'Opera
Seria** (Italy); **Play/Not I** (BAC); **House
Of The Gods** (MTW/Royal Opera
House 2); **Restoration** (Bristol Old
Vic, Headlong Theatre); **Betrayal**
(nominated Best Design, Scottish
Critics Awards 2012) (Glasgow
Citizens); Sondheim's **Sweeney Todd**
(TMA Best Musical Production 2010,
nominated Best Design, Scottish
Critics awards 2011) (Dundee Rep
Theatre); **Europe** (Barbican); **Betrayal**
(The Crucible, Sheffield); **La Boheme**
(Opera Holland Park, Kensington);
The Caucasian Chalk Circle (Shared
Experience/WYP/Nottingham
Playhouse); **The Three Musketeers
and The Princess of Spain** (English
Touring Theatre/Traverse/Coventry);
Futureproof (EdinburghTraverse/
Dundee Rep. Winner Scotsman
fringe first 2011); **Men Should Weep**
(National Theatre of Scotland); **The
Lieutenant of Inishmore** (Royal
Lyceum, Edinburgh); **The Matchbox**
(Liverpool Everyman, Playhouse)
and **James and the Giant Peach**
(Birmingham Stage Company,
National Tour).
Television credits include: first series
and pre-production assistant designer
on **Doctor Who**.
Future work includes: **Titus
Andronicus** (RSC); **The Pearl Fishers**
(Opera Holland Park); **Beautiful
Thing** (West End/National Tour);
Wendy and Peter Pan (RSC) and
The Matchbox (Tricycle Theatre,
London).

TIM MITCHELL Lighting Designer
Previous productions for West
Yorkshire Playhouse include **The
History Boys**.
Tim is an Associate Lighting Designer
for the Royal Shakespeare Company
and Chichester Festival Theatre. His
many credits include: **Kiss Me Kate**
(Old Vic/Chichester); **A Chorus of
Disapproval** (West End); **My Fair
Lady** (Sheffield); **Singin' in the Rain**
(Nominated for Best Musical Revival
Olivier Award, West End/Chichester);
Crazy For You (West End/Regents
Park); **Written on the Heart** (West
End/RSC); **The Lion, the Witch
and the Wardrobe** (Kensington
Gardens); **Goodnight Mr. Tom**/
Yes Prime Minister (West End/UK
Tour/Chichester); **Rosencrantz and
Guildenstern are Dead** (West End/
Chichester); **The Orphan of Zhao**,
The City Madam, **Cardenio**, **Morte
D'Arthur** (RSC); **Lend Me A Tenor**
(West End/Plymouth); **Earthquakes
in London** (Headlong); **Smash**
(Menier); **Forests**, **The Cherry
Orchard** (Birmingham Rep); **The
Three Musketeers** (Rose Theatre);
Tell Me on A Sunday (Tour); **Master
Class** (Theatre Royal Bath); **Filumena,
The Knot of the Heart**, **Becky
Shaw** (Almeida); **The Resistable
Rise of Arturo Ui**, **The Syndicate,
The CriticReal Inspector Hound,
Bingo** (Chichester Festival Theatre);
Dirty Dancing (West End/Toronto/
Hamburg/Utrecht/USABerlin/
South Africa); **Alphabetical Order,
Darker Shores**, **Amongst Friends**
(Hampstead); **A Month in the
Country** (Salisbury); **Sleeping Beauty**
(New York/Barbican/Young Vic);
Henry IV Parts I & II (Shakespeare
Theatre, Washington); **The Play
What I Wrote** (Broadway/West End);
Merrily We Roll Along (Donmar) and
Hamlet (Japan/Sadler's Wells).
Opera and Ballet credits include: **La
Boheme, Die Fledermause** (WNO);
A Streetcar Named Desire (Scottish
Ballet); **Die Frau Ohne Schatten,
Elektra** (Mariinsky Theatre, Russia/
Opera de Nice) and **Ariadne Auf
Naxos** (WNO/Boston).

DAN JONES Composer
and Sound Designer
Previous work with Dominic Hill includes:
Happy Days, **A Midsummer Night's Dream**, **Peter Pan** (Dundee Rep); **The City Madam** and **Fall** (RSC).
Other Theatre credits include: **Antigone**, **The Kitchen**, **Greenland** (National Theatre); Tim Crouch's **England** (WhitechapelNational Theatre); **I Cinna**, **Ivan and the Dogs** (ATCSohoRustaveli Theatre Tbilisi); **King Lear**, **The House of Bernarda Alba**, **Knot of the Heart**, **Through a Glass Darkly** (Almeida); **Kursk** (Prague Quadrennial Special Prize for Sound Design); **War Music**, **The Watery Part of the World**, **Going Dark** (Sound&Fury); **A Prayer for My Daughter** (Young Vic); **Slippage** (Rambert); **Othello**, **Krapp's Last Tape**, **A Kind of Alaska**, **The Turn of the Screw**, **Uncle Vanya** (Bristol Old Vic) and **Coriolanus**, **The Changeling**, **The Taming of the Shrew**, **Julius Caesar**, **The Tempest** (Shakespeare at the Tobacco Factory).
Film credits include: **Max** (Ivor Novello Award Best Film Score); **Shadow of the Vampire**, **Manolete**, **Tomorrow La Scala**, **In Tranzit**, **White Lilacs**, **Four Last Songs**, **Twockers**, **Turn It Loose** and **The Dark Half**.
Television credits include: **The Fear**, **The Town**, **The Secret of Crickley Hall**, **Appropriate Adult**, **Any Human Heart** (Ivor Novello and BAFTA Best Music awards), **Criminal Justice** (2009); **Dead Set**; **David Attenborough's Darwin and the Tree of Life**; **Sahara**; **The Spectre of Hope**, **Secret Lives**; **The Spying Game**; **Wildlife on One**; **The Ghosts of Rwanda**; **The Natural World**; **David Attenborough's Life of Mammals**; **Horizon: The Search for Longitude** and **The Iron Duke**.
Radio credits include: **Between the Ears**: **Down Red Lane** (BBC Radio 3).
Audio artwork and installations include: **Sky Orchestra** (London Olympics 2012, Fierce Festival, RSC Complete Works Festival, Sydney Festival); **Music for Seven Ice Cream Vans** (LIFT, NNF10); **Dream Director** (ICA) and **Listening Posts** (Cork Harbour).
Dan's directing work includes **Going Dark**, **War Music** and **Kursk** (Young Vic and Sydney Opera House) for Sound&Fury Theatre Company which he co-founded and for whom he is an artistic director.

JAMES FREEDMAN Illusion Designer
James Freedman is a British professional magician and magic consultant. He was born in London in 1965 and was introduced to magic when his parents gave him a "Merit Magic Set" for his fourth birthday. This childhood interest grew into a lifelong study of all kinds of magic, illusion and other less honest deceptions. As a teenager, he witnessed child pickpockets on the streets of Paris and decided to become an honest pickpocket. He is now regarded as an expert and is the only person to have secretly picked the pockets of the Mayor of London, The Chancellor of the Exchequer and The Governor of The Bank of England, earning the nickname "The Man of Steal".
Offstage, James works as a specialist adviser for film, television and theatre, designing illusions and teaching actors his unusual skills. He was Illusion Designer on two series of the German show "**Trickfabrik**", winning an Intermedia-Globe-Silver-Award at the WorldMediaFestival in 2010. Freedman is a previous recipient of The Close-Up Magician of the Year Award for his sleight of hand performances and was promoted to membership of The Inner Magic Circle "in recognition of his outstanding abilities as a performer."
Films include: **Les Misérables** (Pickpocket Consultant); **The Illusionist** (Magic Consultant), **Oliver Twist** (Pickpocket Trainer) and **The Brothers Bloom** (Magic Adviser).
Television credits include: **Hustle**, **The Big Breakfast**, **This Morning**, **The Making of Oliver Twist**, **The Real Hustle**, **The Slammer**, **Dip** and **The Gadget Show**.
Theatre credits include: **Magic at the Palladium**, **Wait until Dark** and **The Magic Circle Christmas Show**.

BEN HART Illusion Designer
Ben Hart is a magician and illusion designer for the stage, television, advertising and film. He has developed hundreds of magic tricks and special effects and has performed in America, South Africa, Europe and across the UK. He is a member of The Magic Circle and a past winner of the Young Magician of the Year Award (2007/09). Ben invents, writes and builds magic tricks for magicians, working behind the scenes with some of the world's top performers.

Theatrical Illusion design credits include: **The Arthur Conan Doyle Appreciation Society** (Traverse); **Paul Merton: Out of my Head** (Tour/West End); **Chris Cox Fatal Distraction** (Tour); **Wet Paint Magic Show, StageFright** (Theatre Royal Bury St. Edmunds); **Fatherland** (The Gate); **Wonderland** (Work of Genius) and **Darker Shores** (Hampstead Theatre).

Advertising work for brands including: **Nicorette, Sky TV** and **Trident**.

Work for film and Television includes: **The Egg Trick, The Sorcerer's Apprentice** and **The Dare**.

KALLY LLOYD-JONES
Movement Director
Kally Lloyd-Jones trained as a dancer in Glasgow and Central School of Ballet, London, has an MA in English Literature and Film Studies from Glasgow University and has worked as a director, choreographer, dancer, movement director and teacher in the UK and internationally. In 2012 Kally Lloyd-Jones was awarded a Herald Angel for her directing of **The Seven Deadly Sins**, a Company Chordelia and Scottish Opera co-production. Recent directing credits include **Katya Kabanova** for Scottish, Opera, **Eugene Onegin** for Bloomsbury Opera & St Andrews Opera, **The Rape of Lucretia** for St Andrews Opera, **MacPherson's Rant** for the Byre Theatre, **Thrashing the Sea God** for Tête a Tête Opera Festival) and Opera Scenes for The Royal Conservatoire of Scotland where she also teaches physical performance. She is Artistic Director of Company Chordelia and has recently created, directed and toured the company's latest productions, Les Amoureux, Cabaret Chordelia and Miranda. Her choreography/movement direction credits include **La Bohème, Die Fledermaus, Cinderella, A Night at the Chinese Opera, The Two Widows, The Secret Marriage, Five:15, An Italian Girl in Algiers, The Marriage of Figaro, Rigoletto, Hansel and Gretel, The Magic Flute, The Lady From The Sea** and **Orlando** (Scottish Opera); **A Midsummer Night's Dream, Don Giovanni, The Love For Three Oranges, The Tales of Hoffmann, War and Peace** and **Betrothal in a Monastery** (RCS); **Making Arrangements** and **Amerika** (Tête a Tête Opera); **Green Whale, Wee Witches** (Licketyspit Theatre Company); **The Last Witch** (EIF/Traverse/Lyceum).

CAMILLA EVANS CDG Casting Director

Theatre credits include: **Noises Off** (UK & Ireland Tour – Old Vic); **Hitchcock Blonde (**Hull Truck); **24 Hour Musicals** (Old Vic Gala); **Marriage, Stars In the Morning Sky, Nora, Too Much Pressure**, **One Night In November** (Belgrade); **Three Sisters** (Young Vic); **Taking Part, After The Party** (Criterion); **Boys, Clockwork, Nicked** (Soho Theatre – Hightide Festival 2012); **A Few Man Fridays** (Riverside Studios); **The Diary Of Anne Frank** (York Theatre Royal and Tour); **Cinderella** (Tobacco Factory); **Treasure Island** (Bristol Old Vic); **Crawling In The Dark, The Door Never Closes** (Almeida); **Yerma** (WYP); **Chinglish** (UK casting Goodman Theatre Chicago & Broadway) and **Marine Parade, By Simon Stevens** (Brighton Festival 2010).

Recent Television and Film credits include: **Hustle, Alia Broken, Children's casting with Maggie Lunn, The Heart Fails Without Warning by Hilary Mantel, Trading Licks, Eliminate: Archie Cookson and Scooterman.**

ANDREW WHYMENT
Assistant Director (Birkbeck Trainee)

Andrew is a Theatre Directing MFA student at Birkbeck College and is a Film & Theatre BA Honours First Class graduate from the University of Reading. Andrew is a director, writer and performer. In 2009, he formed his company, Squint.

Recent directorial credits include: **Scratchbook**: **Six Boroughs** (London Bridge Festival); **Broken News** (New Wimbledon Theatre); **Scratchbook: Love Thy Neighbour** (Cockpit Theatre); **Gold & Popcorn** (Old Vic Tunnels); **A Festival Guide** (South Hill Park & Dalston Roof Park) and **Bluebird** (National Tour).

Recent assisting credits include: **Wind in the Willows**, **Cat on a Hot Tin Roof** (West Yorkshire Playhouse); **Our Days of Rage** (Old Vic Tunnels) and **S'warm** (National Youth Theatre).

Andrew is an Associate Director at the National Youth Theatre, working regularly as an assistant director, practitioner and facilitator for the company. Andrew has facilitated workshops for the Shakespeare Schools Festival and Old Vic New Voices. He has also led cultural exchange workshops in China and Saudi Arabia.

WYPLAY HOUSE

WEST YORKSHIRE PLAYHOUSE

West Yorkshire Playhouse is a producing house making vital theatre in Leeds. We are a cultural hub for the city and beyond, a place where people and communities come to tell and share stories; to engage in world class theatre that is pioneering, invigorating and relevant. We seek out the best companies and individual artists locally, nationally and internationally to create inspirational theatre here in the heart of Yorkshire.

We are dedicated collaborators, working regularly with other theatres from across the UK, independent producers and some of the most distinctive, original talent around. We develop work with established practitioners and find new voices that we believe should be heard, providing a creative space for new writers, emerging companies and individual theatre makers. We make work with national and international ambitions yet we're locally rooted and our distinctiveness is informed by where we're from.

Cultural organisations are vital for growth. By opening up our building, our work and our imagination we will develop theatre across many platforms from large-scale spectacle to more intimate performances. We will help transform the way our city is seen. And we will transform the way we see our city, Yorkshire, the world and each other by reaching out to and working with communities, schools and audiences. We are an agent for change, enabling people to develop the skills they need to transform their chances in life, to realise their potential.

We will tell important stories that make a difference, are necessary and are vital for today.

West Yorkshire Playhouse – Vital Theatre

Find us on Facebook: westyorkshireplayhouse
Find us on Twitter: @WYPlayhouse
Wyp.org.uk

CITIZENS THEATRE

"As theatrical icons go, few come bigger than Glasgow's Citizens Theatre" *Herald*

The Citizens Theatre is an iconic venue and theatre company based in the Gorbals area of Glasgow. It has been one of Scotland's flagship producing theatres since 1945, recognised internationally as a leader in its field. Fondly known as The Citz, it is led by Artistic Director, Dominic Hill.

Within a beautiful Victorian auditorium that dates from 1878, the Citizens presents a world-class, contemporary repertoire based on British and foreign classics and new writing. The theatre has extensive backstage workshop facilities where we make all of our own sets and costumes.

As our name suggests, we believe our work can enhance and transform the lives of citizens of all ages, cultures and social backgrounds. We believe that everyone should have the opportunity to take part in the creative life of our theatre, developing skills and self-confidence in an inclusive environment where new friendships can flourish. We are passionate about everything that we offer our audiences, from work on stage to participatory projects. Every week of the year our Citizens Learning team run activities for children, young people, students, older people and families as well as working closely with marginalised groups, people with additional support needs, and in disadvantaged communities across Scotland.

With the expertise of the many artists, writers and actors we collaborate with, our ambition is to provide unique and memorable cultural experiences for our audiences.

For the latest information on all our shows, and to find out how you can take part, visit us online at **citz.co.uk**

Join the conversation
Leave your comments and star ratings on our website

Find us on Facebook: citizenstheatre

Follow us on Twitter @citizenstheatre

Citizens Theatre, 119 Gorbals Street, Glasgow, G5 9DS
0141 429 0022 | citz.co.uk

PROGRAMME NOTES *DOCTOR FAUSTUS*

Christopher Marlowe, like Shakespeare who was born in the same year, is a good example of sixteenth century social mobility; a playwright of humble origins, like Faustus 'his parents base of stock', who rose to move in circles of the rich and powerful, becoming one of the most popular dramatists of his time. Despite his celebrity, however, Marlowe was ever the outsider; possibly spying on the circles he infiltrated, constantly at odds with the law, variously accused of homosexuality, blasphemy and atheism. His short and violent life famously ended in murder (or possibly assassination) in a house in Deptford in 1593. His death was probably connected to his other career as an intelligence gatherer.

Nothing about Marlowe is certain. Many of the more colourful details of his life come from men with agendas: rivals, propagandists, victims of torture. His play, *Doctor Faustus* is no different; it is not known exactly when it was written and the play-text is just as unstable as any of the testimonies from its author's life. Indeed, no one can be sure what version of the play the first audiences saw or how this might have differed from later productions and printed editions.

Plays in the sixteenth century were the movies of their time. Going to the theatre was a popular and affordable pastime, but while drama may have enjoyed large audiences, it was not viewed as a serious art form and plays were not widely available in print. The first edition of *The Tragicall Historie of D Faustus* was not published until 1604, eleven years after Marlowe's death. The 1604 edition is often referred to as the A-text. The second main version, *The tragicall history of the life and death of Doctor Faustus,* published in 1616, is known as the B-text and is much longer. It has more comic scenes and more 'special effects', leading scholars to suggest that the B-text was performed in London playhouses, while the A-text may have been used for touring to venues that couldn't accommodate the more elaborate stage directions of the 1616 text. There were seven other editions of the play published between 1604 and 1631 all with minor variations on either the A or B-text.

Textual integrity is further compromised by the fact that Elizabethan plays were vetted. It has been suggested that some of *Doctor Faustus'* structural defects are the result of such censorship. These 'defects' have aroused a great deal of debate. The central comic scenes of the 1616 text in particular have been criticised as marring a great play and are viewed by some critics as later insertions not written by Marlowe. It is possible they are the 'adicyones in doctor fostes' that the theatrical manager Philip

Henslowe paid William Birde and Samuel Rowley for in 1602. They got £4 for their work. The lengthy scenes involving Pope Adrian and his rival, Bruno, were clearly designed to appease the English public's hostility towards Roman Catholicism. The Pope had excommunicated Elizabeth I, proclaiming in 1580 that it would not be a mortal sin to assassinate her. England was also at war with Catholic nations abroad, most notably Spain. Setting a greedy pope and his cardinals up for some slapstick retribution in the form of food gags must have gone down well at the Rose playhouse in London. While these comic episodes may express the 'carnivalesque', they do little to further the action of the play or develop the characters.

Colin Teevan, in his 'additions', plays on the motifs of espionage and spectacle that abound in Doctor Faustus; but where Faustus spies on the pope in the early texts, now he is spied on by secret service goons. In Marlowe's play Doctor Faustus appears to sell his soul for little more than to play the part of a court magician, conjuring out-of-season grapes for duchesses and simulated heroes for emperors. Teevan elaborates on the idea of evil as empty spectacle by placing his new scenes backstage at Faustus' conjuring show. Faustus is a modern day 'Master of Concealed Arts' playing venues across the world, from Paris to Las Vegas to Trier. Mephistopheles, despite acting as conjuror's assistant, still maintains the upper hand, dissuading Faustus from a potentially redemptive love (itself an allusion to Goethe's nineteenth century Faust).

Doctor Faustus is a play that raises many questions, not only regarding the views of its author (possible government spy and atheist) but also in terms of its themes, genre and characterisation. Is it a morality tale, warning against the seductive powers of pride and avarice or do we end up sympathising with Faustus as a tragic hero who, like Marlowe himself, is a Renaissance everyman punished for stretching knowledge to its limits?

According to the scholar Stephen Greenblatt, 'Marlowe writes in the period in which European man embarked on his extraordinary career of consumption, his eager pursuit of knowledge, with one intellectual model after another seized, squeezed dry, and discarded, and his frenzied exhaustion of the world's resources.'[1] Images of greed recur throughout the play; Faustus by his own admission is 'glutted with conceit'. Teevan's contemporary scenes show us just how relevant Faustus' desires and dilemmas still are in our own age of globalisation, mass consumption and celebrity adulation.

Madeline Dewhurst, The Open University

(Endnotes)
1   Stephen Grrenblatt, *Renaissance Self-Fashioning: From More to Shakespeare* (Chicago: The University of Chicago Press, 1980), p.199.

DOCTOR FAUSTUS

Christopher Marlowe
and Colin Teevan

DOCTOR FAUSTUS

OBERON BOOKS
LONDON

WWW.OBERONBOOKS.COM

First published in 2013 by Oberon Books Ltd
521 Caledonian Road, London N7 9RH
Tel: +44 (0) 20 7607 3637 / Fax: +44 (0) 20 7607 3629
e-mail: info@oberonbooks.com
www.oberonbooks.com

A catalogue record for this book is available from the British Library.

PB ISBN: 978-1-84943-413-3
E ISBN: 978-1-84943-798-1

Cover design by Freight Design

Printed, bound and converted
by CPI Group (UK) Ltd, Croydon, CR0 4YY.

Characters

DR FAUSTUS

WAGNER

GOOD ANGEL

EVIL ANGEL

CORNELIUS

VALDES

MEPHISTOPHELES

LUCIFER

SAXON BRUNO

ROBYN

POPE

PRESIDENT

DUCHESS

CHORUS also play:

DEVIL'S SERVANT

SEVEN DEADLY SINS

BANKER, MEDIA MOGUL and MINISTER

THE QUEEN

MARILYN MONROE

ABRAHAM LINCOLN

SECRET SERVICE MAN and SWAT TEAM

DUKE

FIRST, SECOND and THIRD SCHOLARS

SCENE 1

Enter CHORUS.

CHORUS

Not marching now in fields of Trasimene,
Where Mars did mate the Carthaginians,
Nor sporting in the dalliance of love,
In courts of kings where state is overturned,
Nor in the pomp of proud audacious deeds,
Intends our muse to daunt his heavenly verse.
Only this, gentlemen: we must perform
The form of Faustus' fortunes, good or bad.
And now to patient judgments we appeal,
And speak for Faustus in his infancy,
Now is he born, his parents base of stock,
In Germany, within a town called Rhode.
Of riper years to Wittenberg he went,
Whereas his kinsmen chiefly brought him up.
So soon he profits in divinity,
The fruitful plot of scholarism graced,
That shortly he was graced with doctor's name,
Excelling all, and sweetly can dispute
In heavenly matters of theology;
Till, swoll'n with cunning of a self-conceit,
His waxen wings did mount above his reach,
And melting heavens conspired his overthrow.
For, falling to a devilish exercise,
And glutted now with learning's golden gifts,
He surfeits upon cursèd necromancy;
Nothing so sweet as magic is to him,
Which he prefers before his chiefest bliss,
And this the man that in his study sits.

Exit.

SCENE 2

FAUSTUS

Settle thy studies, Faustus, and begin
To sound the depth of that thou wilt profess.
Having commenced, be a divine in show,
Yet level at the end of every art,
And live and die in Aristotle's works;
Sweet Analytics, 'tis thou hast ravished me!
(He reads.)
'Bene disserere est finis logices.'
Is to dispute well logic's chiefest end?
Affords this art no greater miracle?
Then read no more. Thou hast attained the end.
A greater subject fitteth Faustus' wit.
Bid *On kai me* on farewell. Galen, come!
Be a physician, Faustus. Heap up gold,
And be eternised for some wondrous cure.
(He reads.)
'Summum bonum medicinae sanitas.'
The end of physic is our body's health.
Why Faustus, hast thou not attained that end?
Is not thy common talk sound aphorisms?
Are not thy bills hung up as monuments,
Whereby whole cities have escaped the plague
And thousand desp'rate maladies been eased?
Yet art thou still but Faustus, and a man.
Wouldst thou make man to live eternally?
Or, being dead, raise them to life again?
Then this profession were to be esteemed.
Physic, farewell! Where is Justinian?
(He reads.)
'Si una eademque res legatur duobus,
Alter rem, alter valorem rei', etc.
A pretty case of paltry legacies!
(He reads.)
'Exhaereditare filium non potest pater nisi' –
Such is the subject of the institute
And universal body of the Church.
His study fits a mercenary drudge,

Who aims at nothing but external trash –
Too servile and illiberal for me.
When all is done, divinity is best.
Jerome's Bible, Faustus, view it well.
    (He reads.)
'Stipendium peccati mors est.' Ha!
'Stipendium', etc.
The reward of sin is death. That's hard.
    (He reads.)
'Si peccasse negamus, fallimur
Et nulla est in nobis veritas.'
If we say that we have no sin,
We deceive ourselves, and there's no truth in us.
Why then belike we must sin,
And so consequently die.
Ay, we must die an everlasting death.
What doctrine call you this, *Che serà, serà,*
What will be, shall be? Divinity, adieu!
    (He picks up a book of magic.)
These metaphysics of magicians
And necromantic books are heavenly:
Lines, circles, signs, letters, and characters –
Ay, these are those that Faustus most desires.
O, what a world of profit and delight,
Of power, of honour, of omnipotence,
Is promised to the studious artisan!
All things that move between the quiet poles
Shall be at my command. Emperors and kings
Are but obeyed in their several provinces,
Nor can they raise the wind or rend the clouds;
But his dominion that exceeds in this
Stretcheth as far as doth the mind of man.
A sound magician is a mighty god.
Here, Faustus, tire thy brains to gain a deity.
Wagner!

    Enter WAGNER.

FAUSTUS
Commend me to my dearest friends,
The German Valdes and Cornelius.
Request them earnestly to visit me.

WAGNER
I will, sir.

Exit WAGNER.

FAUSTUS
Their conference will be a greater help to me
Than all my labours, plod I ne'er so fast.

Enter the GOOD ANGEL and the EVIL ANGEL.

GOOD ANGEL
O Faustus, lay that damnèd book aside,
And gaze not on it, lest it tempt thy soul,
And heap God's heavy wrath upon thy head.
Read, read the Scriptures. That is blasphemy.

EVIL ANGEL
Go forward, Faustus, in that famous art
Wherein all nature's treasury is contained.
Be thou on earth as Jove is in the sky;
Lord and commander of these elements.

Exit ANGELS.

FAUSTUS
How am I glutted with conceit of this!
Shall I make spirits fetch me what I please,
Resolve me of all ambiguities,
Perform what desperate enterprise I will?
I'll have them fly to India for gold,
Ransack the ocean for orient pearl,
And search all corners of the new-found world
For pleasant fruits and princely delicates.
I'll have them read me strange philosophy,
And tell the secrets of all foreign kings.
I'll have them wall all Germany with brass
And make swift Rhine circle fair Wittenberg.
I'll levy soldiers with the coin they bring,

And chase the Prince of Parma from our land,
And reign sole king of all our provinces.
Come, German Valdes and Cornelius,
And make me blest with your sage conference!

Enter VALDES and CORNELIUS.

FAUSTUS
Valdes, sweet Valdes, and Cornelius,
Know that your words have won me at the last,
To practice magic and concealèd arts.
Yet, not your words only, but mine own fantasy,
That will receive no object, for my head,
But ruminates on necromantic skill.
Philosophy is odious and obscure,
Both law and physic are for petty wits;
Divinity is basest of the three,
Unpleasant, harsh, contemptible, and vile:
'Tis magic, magic that hath ravished me.
Then, gentle friends, aid me in this attempt.

VALDES
Faustus, these books, thy wit, and our experience
Shall make all nations to canonize us.
As Indian Moors obey their Spanish lords,
So shall the subjects of every element
Be always serviceable to us three.
Like lions shall they guard us when we please,
Like Almaine rutters with their horsemen's staves,
Or Lapland giants, trotting by our sides;
Sometimes like women, or unwedded maids,
Shadowing more beauty in their airy brows
Than in the white breasts of the Queen of Love.
From Venice shall they drag huge argosies,
And from America the golden fleece,
That yearly stuffs old Philip's treasury,
If learnèd Faustus will be resolute.

FAUSTUS
Valdes, as resolute am I in this
As thou to live; therefore object it not.

CORNELIUS

The miracles that magic will perform
Will make thee vow to study nothing else.
He that is grounded in astrology,
Enriched with tongues, well seen in minerals,
Hath all the principles magic doth require.
Then doubt not, Faustus, but to be renowned
And more frequented for this mystery
Than heretofore the Delphian oracle.
The spirits tell me they can dry the sea,
And fetch the treasure of all foreign wrecks –
Ay, all the wealth that our forefathers hid
Within the massy entrails of the earth.
Then tell me, Faustus, what shall we three want?

FAUSTUS

Nothing, Cornelius. O, this cheers my soul!
Come, show me some demonstrations magical,
That I may conjure in some lusty grove,
And have these joys in full possession.

VALDES

Then haste thee to some solitary grove,
And bear wise Bacon's and Albanus' works,
The Hebrew Psalter, and New Testament;
And whatsoever else is requisite
We will inform thee ere our conference cease.

CORNELIUS

Valdes, first let him know the words of art,
And then, all other ceremonies learned,
Faustus may try his cunning by himself.

VALDES

First I'll instruct thee in the rudiments,
And then wilt thou be perfecter than I.

FAUSTUS

Then come and dine with me, and after meat
We'll canvass every quiddity thereof,
For ere I sleep I'll try what I can do.
This night I'll conjure, though I die therefore.

Exit all.

SCENE 3

FAUSTUS
Now that the gloomy shadow of the earth,
Longing to view Orion's drizzling look,
Leaps from th'Antarctic world unto the sky,
And dims the welkin with her pitchy breath,
Faustus, begin thine incantations,
And try if devils will obey thy hest,
Seeing thou hast prayed and sacrificed to them.

He draws a circle.

FAUSTUS
Within this circle is Jehovah's name,
Forward and backward anagrammatised,
The breviated names of holy saints,
Figures of every adjunct to the heavens,
And characters of signs and erring stars,
By which the spirits are enforced to rise.
Then fear not, Faustus, but be resolute,
And try the uttermost magic can perform.
Sint mihi dei Acherontis propitii! Valeat numen triplex Jehovae! Ignei, aerii, aquatici, terreni, spiritus, salvete! Orientis princeps Lucifer, Beelzebub, inferni ardentis monarcha, et Demogorgon, propitiamus vos, ut appareat et surgat Mephistopheles! Quid tumoraris? Per Jehovam, Gehennam, et consecratam aquam quam nunc spargo, signumque crucis quod nunc facio, et per vota nostra, Ipse nunc surgat nobis dicatus Mephistopheles!

Enter a DEVIL (MEPHISTOPHELES).

FAUSTUS
I charge thee to return and change thy shape.
Thou art too ugly to attend on me.
Go, and return an old Franciscan friar;
That holy shape becomes a devil best.

Exit DEVIL (MEPHISTOPHELES).

FAUSTUS
I see there's virtue in my heavenly words.
Who would not be proficient in this art?

How pliant is this Mephistopheles –
Full of obedience and humility –
Such is the force of magic and my spells!
Now, Faustus, thou art conjuror laureate,
That canst command great Mephistopheles.
Quin redis, Mephistopheles, fratris imagine!

    Re-enter MEPHISTOPHELES disguised.

MEPHISTOPHELES
Now, Faustus, what wouldst thou have me do?

FAUSTUS
I charge thee wait upon me whilst I live,
To do whatever Faustus shall command,
Be it to make the moon drop from her sphere,
Or the ocean to overwhelm the world.

MEPHISTOPHELES
I am a servant to great Lucifer
And may not follow thee without his leave.
No more than he commands must we perform.

FAUSTUS
Did not he charge thee to appear to me?

MEPHISTOPHELES
No, I came hither of mine own accord.

FAUSTUS
Did not my conjuring speeches raise thee? Speak.

MEPHISTOPHELES
That was the cause, but yet *per accidens.*
For when we hear one rack the name of God,
Abjure the Scriptures and his Saviour Christ,
We fly in hope to get his glorious soul;
Nor will we come unless he use such means
Whereby he is in danger to be damned.
Therefore, the shortest cut for conjuring
Is stoutly to abjure the Trinity,
And pray devoutly to the prince of hell.

FAUSTUS

So Faustus hath
Already done, and holds this principle:
There is no chief but only Beelzebub,
To whom Faustus doth dedicate himself.
This word 'damnation' terrifies not him,
For he confounds hell in Elysium.
His ghost be with the old philosophers!
But leaving these vain trifles of men's souls,
Tell me what is that Lucifer thy lord?

MEPHISTOPHELES

Arch-regent and commander of all spirits.

FAUSTUS

Was not that Lucifer an angel once?

MEPHISTOPHELES

Yes, Faustus, and most dearly loved of God.

FAUSTUS

How comes it then that he is prince of devils?

MEPHISTOPHELES

O, by aspiring pride and insolence,
For which God threw him from the face of heaven.

FAUSTUS

And what are you that live with Lucifer?

MEPHISTOPHELES

Unhappy spirits that fell with Lucifer,
Conspired against our God with Lucifer,
And are for ever damned with Lucifer.

FAUSTUS

Where are you damned?

MEPHISTOPHELES

In hell.

FAUSTUS

How comes it then that thou art out of hell?

MEPHISTOPHELES

Why, this is hell, nor am I out of it.
Think'st thou that I, who saw the face of God
And tasted the eternal joys of heaven,
Am not tormented with ten thousand hells,
In being deprived of everlasting bliss?
O Faustus, leave these frivolous demands,
Which strike a terror to my fainting soul!

FAUSTUS

What, is great Mephistopheles so passionate
For being deprivèd of the joys of heaven?
Learn thou of Faustus' manly fortitude,
And scorn those joys thou never shalt possess.
Go bear these tidings to great Lucifer:
Seeing Faustus hath incurred eternal death,
By desp'rate thoughts against Jove's deity,
Say he surrenders up to him his soul,
So he will spare him four-and-twenty years,
Letting him live in all voluptuousness,
Having thee ever to attend on me,
To give me whatsoever I shall ask,
To tell me whatsoever I demand,
To slay mine enemies, and aid my friends,
And always be obedient to my will.
Go and return to mighty Lucifer,
And meet me in my study at midnight,
And then resolve me of thy master's mind.

MEPHISTOPHELES

I will, Faustus.

Exit MEPHISTOPHELES.

FAUSTUS

Had I as many souls as there be stars,
I'd give them all for Mephistopheles.
By her I'll be great emperor of the world,
And make a bridge through the moving air
To pass the ocean with a band of men;
I'll join the hills that bind the Afric shore
And make that land continent to Spain,

And both contributory to my crown.
The Emp'ror shall not live but by my leave,
Nor any potentate of Germany.
Now that I have obtained what I desire,
I'll live in speculation of this art
Till Mephistopheles return again.

SCENE 4

FAUSTUS
Now, Faustus, must thou needs be damned,
And canst thou not be saved?
What boots it then to think of God or heaven?
Away with such vain fancies and despair!
Despair in God and trust in Beelzebub.
Now go not backward: no, Faustus, be resolute.
Why waverest thou? O, something soundeth in mine ears:
'Abjure this magic, turn to God again!'
Ay, and Faustus will turn to God again.
To God? He loves thee not.
The god thou servest is thine own appetite,
Wherein is fixed the love of Beelzebub.
To him I'll build an altar and a church,
And offer lukewarm blood of new-born babes.

Enter the GOOD ANGEL and the EVIL ANGEL.

GOOD ANGEL
Sweet Faustus, leave that execrable art.

FAUSTUS
Contrition, prayer, repentance – what of them?

GOOD ANGEL
O, they are means to bring thee unto heaven.

EVIL ANGEL
Rather illusions, fruits of lunacy,
That makes men foolish that do trust them most.

GOOD ANGEL
Sweet Faustus, think of heaven and heavenly things.

EVIL ANGEL
No, Faustus; think of honour and of wealth.

Exit ANGELS.

FAUSTUS
Of wealth?
Why, the seigniory of Emden shall be mine.
When Mephistopheles shall stand by me,

What god can hurt thee, Faustus? Thou art safe;
Cast no more doubts. Come, Mephistopheles,
And bring glad tidings from great Lucifer.
Is't not midnight? Come, Mephistopheles!
Veni, veni, Mephistophile!

Enter MEPHISTOPHELES.

FAUSTUS
Now tell, what says Lucifer, thy lord?

MEPHISTOPHELES
That I shall wait on Faustus whilst he lives,
So he will buy my service with his soul.

FAUSTUS
Already Faustus hath hazarded that for thee.

MEPHISTOPHELES
But, Faustus, thou must bequeath it solemnly,
And write a deed of gift with thine own blood,
For that security craves great Lucifer.
If thou deny it, I will back to hell.

FAUSTUS
Stay, Mephistopheles, and tell me, what good will my soul do thy
lord?

MEPHISTOPHELES
Enlarge his kingdom.

FAUSTUS
Is that the reason why he tempts us thus?

MEPHISTOPHELES
Solamen miseris socios habuisse doloris.
Misery loves company.

FAUSTUS
Have you any pain that tortures other?

MEPHISTOPHELES
As great as have the human souls of men.
But tell me, Faustus, shall I have thy soul?
And I will be thy slave, and wait on thee,
And give thee more than thou hast wit to ask.

FAUSTUS
Ay, Mephistopheles, I'll give it thee.

MEPHISTOPHELES
Then stab thine arm courageously,
And bind thy soul that at some certain day
Great Lucifer may claim it as his own,
And then be thou as great as Lucifer.

FAUSTUS cuts his arm.

FAUSTUS
Lo, Mephistopheles, for love of thee
I cut mine arm, and with my proper blood
Assure my soul to be great Lucifer's,
Chief lord and regent of perpetual night.
View here the blood that trickles from mine arm,
And let it be propitious for my wish.

MEPHISTOPHELES
But Faustus, thou must write it in manner of a deed of gift.

FAUSTUS
Ay, so I will.
    (He writes.)
          But Mephistopheles,
My blood congeals, and I can write no more.

MEPHISTOPHELES
I'll fetch thee fire to dissolve it straight.

Exit MEPHISTOPHELES.

FAUSTUS
What might the staying of my blood portend?
Is it unwilling I should write this bill?
Why streams it not, that I may write afresh?
'Faustus gives to thee his soul' – ah, there it stayed!
Why shouldst thou not? Is not thy soul thine own?
Then write again: 'Faustus give to thee his soul.'

Enter MEPHISTOPHELES.

MEPHISTOPHELES
Here's fire. Come Faustus, set it on.

FAUSTUS
So, now the blood begins to clear again,
Now will I make an end immediately.

He writes.

MEPHISTOPHELES
(Aside.)
O, what will not I do to obtain his soul?

FAUSTUS
Consummatum est. This bill is ended,
And Faustus hath bequeathed his soul to Lucifer.
But what is this inscription on mine arm?
'Homo, fuge!' Whither should I fly?
If unto God, he'll throw me down to hell –
My senses are deceived; here's nothing writ –

FAUSTUS looks at arm. It is blank. He looks to other arm.

FAUSTUS
I see it plain. Here in this place is writ
'Homo, fuge!' Yet shall not Faustus fly.

MEPHISTOPHELES
(Aside.)
 I'll fetch him somewhat to delight his mind.

Exit. MEPHISTOPHELES returns with DEVILS.

FAUSTUS
Speak, Mephistopheles. What means this show?

MEPHISTOPHELES
Nothing, Faustus, but to delight thy mind withal,
And to show thee what magic can perform.

FAUSTUS
But may I raise up spirits when I please?

MEPHISTOPHELES
Ay, Faustus, and do greater things than these.

FAUSTUS
Then there's enough for a thousand souls.
Here, Mephistopheles, receive this scroll,

A deed of gift of body and of soul –
But yet conditionally that thou perform
All articles prescribed between us both.

MEPHISTOPHELES
Faustus, I swear by hell and Lucifer
To effect all promises between us made.

FAUSTUS
Then hear me read them.
'On these conditions following:
First, that Faustus may be a spirit in form and substance.
Secondly, that Mephistopheles shall be his servant and at his command.
Thirdly, that Mephistopheles shall do for him and bring him whatsoever.
Fourthly, that he shall be in his chamber or house invisible.
Lastly, that he shall appear to the said John Faustus at all times in what form or shape soever he please.
I, John Faustus, of Wittenberg, Doctor, by these presents, do give both body and soul to Lucifer, Prince of the East, and his minister Mephistopheles; and furthermore grant unto them that four-and-twenty years being expired, the articles above written inviolate, full power to fetch or carry the said John Faustus, body and soul, flesh, blood, or goods, into their habitation wheresoever.
By me, John Faustus'

MEPHISTOPHELES
Speak, Faustus. Do you deliver this as your deed?

FAUSTUS
(Giving the deed.)
Ay, take it, and the devil give thee good on't.

MEPHISTOPHELES
Now, Faustus, ask what thou wilt.

FAUSTUS
First will I question with thee about hell.
Tell me, where is the place that men call hell?

MEPHISTOPHELES
Under the heavens.

FAUSTUS
Ay, but where about?

MEPHISTOPHELES
Within the bowels of these elements,
Where we are tortured and remain for ever.
Hell hath no limits, nor is circumscribed
In one self place, for where we are is hell,
And where hell is must we ever be.
And, to conclude, when all the world dissolves,
And every creature shall be purified,
All places shall be hell that are not heaven.

FAUSTUS
Come, I think hell's a fable.

MEPHISTOPHELES
Ay, think so still, till experience change thy mind.

FAUSTUS
Why, think'st thou then that Faustus shall be damned?

MEPHISTOPHELES
Ay, of necessity, for here's the scroll
Wherein thou hast given thy soul to Lucifer.

FAUSTUS
Ay, and body too, but what of that?
Think'st thou that Faustus is so fond
To imagine that after this life there is any pain?
Tush, these are trifles and mere old wives' tales.

MEPHISTOPHELES
But, Faustus, I am an instance to prove the contrary, for I am damned, and am now in hell.

FAUSTUS
How? Now in hell? Nay, and this be hell, I'll willingly be damned here. What? Walking, disputing, etc.? But leaving off this, let me have a wife, the fairest maid in Germany, for I am wanton and lascivious and cannot live without a wife.

MEPHISTOPHELES
How a wife? I prithee, Faustus, talk not of a wife.

FAUSTUS

Nay, sweet Mephistopheles, fetch me one, for I will have one.

MEPHISTOPHELES

Well, thou wilt have one. Sit there till I come. I'll fetch thee a wife, in the devil's name.

Exit MEPHISTOPHELES and return with a DEVIL dressed like a woman, with fireworks.

MEPHISTOPHELES

Tell, Faustus, how dost thou like thy wife?

FAUSTUS

A plague on her for a hot whore!

MEPHISTOPHELES

Tut, Faustus, marriage is but a ceremonial toy.
If thou lovest me, think no more of it.

Exit DEVIL.

MEPHISTOPHELES

I'll cull thee out the fairest courtesans,
And bring them ev'ry morning to thy bed.
She whom thine eye shall like, thy heart shall have,
Be she as chaste as was Penelope,
As wise as Saba, or as beautiful
As was bright Lucifer before his fall.
   (Presenting a book.)
Hold, take this book. Peruse it thoroughly.
The iterating of these lines brings gold;
The framing of this circle on the ground
Brings whirlwinds, tempests, thunder, and lightning.
Pronounce this thrice devoutly to thyself,
And men in armour shall appear to thee,
Ready to execute what thou desir'st.

FAUSTUS

Thanks, Mephistopheles. Yet fain would I have a book wherein I might behold all spells and incantations, that I might raise up spirits when I please.

MEPHISTOPHELES

Here they are in this book.

They turn to them.

FAUSTUS

Now would I have a book where I might see all characters and planets of the heavens, that I might know their motions and dispositions.

MEPHISTOPHELES

Here they are too.

They turn to them.

FAUSTUS

Nay, let me have one book more, and then I have done, wherein I might see all plants, herbs, and trees that grow upon the earth.

MEPHISTOPHELES

Here they be.

They turn to them.

FAUSTUS

O, thou art deceived.

MEPHISTOPHELES

Tut, I warrant thee.

Exit FAUSTUS and MEPHISTOPHELES.

SCENE 5

Enter CHORUS.

CHORUS
Learned Faustus to find the secrets of Astronomy,
Graven in the book of Jove's high firmament,
Did mount him up to scale Olympus' top,
Where sitting in a chariot burning bright,
Drawn by the strength of yoked dragons' necks;
He views the clouds, the planets, and the stars,
The tropic, zones, and quarters of the sky,
From the bright circle of the hornèd moon,
Even to the height of *Primum Mobile.*
And whirling round with this circumference,
Within the concave compass of the pole,
From east to west his dragons swiftly glide,
And in eight days did bring him home again.

Exit CHORUS.

SCENE 6

Enter FAUSTUS and MEPHISTOPHELES.

FAUSTUS
When I behold the heavens, then I repent
And curse thee, wicked Mephistopheles,
Because thou hast deprived me of those joys.

MEPHISTOPHELES
Why, Faustus,
Think'st thou heaven is such a glorious thing?
I tell thee, 'tis not half so fair as thou,
Or any man that breathes on earth.

FAUSTUS
How provest thou that?

MEPHISTOPHELES
It was made for man; therefore is man more excellent.

FAUSTUS
If it were made for man, 'twas made for me.
I will renounce this magic and repent.

Enter the GOOD ANGEL and the EVIL ANGEL.

GOOD ANGEL
Faustus, repent yet, God will pity thee.

EVIL ANGEL
Thou art a spirit, God cannot pity thee.

FAUSTUS
Who buzzeth in mine ears I am a spirit?
Be I a devil, yet God may pity me;
Ay, God will pity me, if I repent.

EVIL ANGEL
Ay, but Faustus never shall repent.

Exit ANGELS.

FAUSTUS
My heart's so hardened I cannot repent.
Scarce can I name salvation, faith, or heaven

But fearful echoes thunder in mine ears:
'Faustus, thou art damned!' Then swords and knives,
Poison, guns, halters, and envenomed steel
Are laid before me to despatch myself;
And long ere this I should have slain myself,
Had not sweet pleasure conquered deep despair.
Have not I made blind Homer sing to me,
Of Alexander's love and Oenone's death?
And hath not he that built the walls of Thebes
With ravishing sound of his melodious harp
Made music with my Mephistopheles?
Why should I die, then, or basely despair?
I am resolved Faustus shall ne'er repent.
Come, Mephistopheles, let us dispute again
And argue of divine astrology.
Tell me, are there many heavens above the moon?
Are all celestial bodies but one globe,
As is the substance of this centric earth?

MEPHISTOPHELES
As are the elements, such are the spheres,
Mutually folded in each others' orb;
And, Faustus, all jointly move upon one axletree,
Whose *termine* is termed the world's wide pole.
Nor are the names of Saturn, Mars, or Jupiter
Feigned, but are erring stars.

FAUSTUS
But, tell me, have they all one motion, both *situ et tempore*?

MEPHISTOPHELES
All jointly move from east to west in four-and-twenty hours upon the poles of the world, but differ in their motion upon the poles of the zodiac.

FAUSTUS
Tush, these slender trifles Wagner can decide.
Hath Mephistopheles no greater skill?
Who knows not the double motion of the planets?
The first is finished in a natural day,
The second thus, as Saturn in thirty years,

Jupiter in twelve, Mars in four, the Sun, Venus, and Mercury in a year, the moon in twenty-eight days. Tush, these are freshmen's suppositions. But tell me, hath every sphere a dominion or *intelligentia*?

MEPHISTOPHELES
Ay.

FAUSTUS
How many heavens or spheres are there?

MEPHISTOPHELES
Nine: the seven planets, the firmament, and the empyreal heaven.

FAUSTUS
Well, resolve me in this question: why have we not conjunctions, oppositions, aspects, eclipses all at one time, but in some years we have more, in some less?

MEPHISTOPHELES
*Per in aequalem motum respectu totu*s.

FAUSTUS
Well, I am answered. Tell me who made the world?

MEPHISTOPHELES
I will not.

FAUSTUS
Sweet Mephistopheles, tell me.

MEPHISTOPHELES
Move me not, for I will not tell thee.

FAUSTUS
Villain, have I not bound thee to tell me anything?

MEPHISTOPHELES
Ay, that is not against our kingdom, but this is. Think thou on hell, Faustus, for thou art damned.

FAUSTUS
Think, Faustus, upon God, that made the world.

MEPHISTOPHELES
Remember this!

Exit MEPHISTOPHELES.

FAUSTUS
Ay, go, accursèd spirit, to ugly hell!
'Tis thou hast damned distressed Faustus' soul.
Is't not too late?

Enter the GOOD ANGEL and the EVIL ANGEL.

EVIL ANGEL
Too late.

GOOD ANGEL
Never too late, if Faustus can repent.

EVIL ANGEL
If thou repent, devils shall tear thee in pieces.

GOOD ANGEL
Repent, and they shall never raze thy skin.

Exit ANGELS.

FAUSTUS
Ah, Christ, my Saviour,
Seek to save distressèd Faustus' soul!

Enter LUCIFER, BEELZEBUB, and MEPHISTOPHELES.

LUCIFER
Christ cannot save thy soul, for he is just.
There's none but I have int'rest in the same.

FAUSTUS
O, who art thou that look'st so terrible?

LUCIFER
I am Lucifer,
And this is my companion prince in hell.

FAUSTUS
O Faustus, they are come to fetch away thy soul!

LUCIFER
We come to tell thee thou dost injure us.
Thou talk'st of Christ, contrary to thy promise.

Thou shouldst not think of God. Think of the devil –
And of his dame, too.

FAUSTUS
Nor will I henceforth. Pardon me in this,
And Faustus vows never to look to heaven,
Never to name God, or to pray to him,
To burn his Scriptures, slay his ministers,
And make my spirits pull his churches down.

LUCIFER
Do so, and we will highly gratify thee. Faustus, we are come from
hell to show thee some pastime. Sit down, and thou shalt see all
the Seven Deadly Sins appear in their proper shapes.

FAUSTUS
That sight will be as pleasing unto me as paradise was to Adam
the first day of his creation.

LUCIFER
Talk not of Paradise, nor creation, but mark this show. Talk of the
devil, and nothing else.
(Calling offstage.)
Come away!

FAUSTUS sits. Enter the SEVEN DEADLY SINS.

LUCIFER
Now, Faustus, examine them of their several names and
dispositions.

FAUSTUS
What art thou, the first?

PRIDE
I am Pride. I disdain to have any parents. I am like a flea: I can
creep into every corner of a wench. Sometimes like a periwig I
sit upon her brow; or like a fan of feathers I kiss her lips. Indeed
I do – what do I not? But fie, what a scent is here! I'll not speak
another word, except the ground were perfumed and covered
with cloth of arras.

FAUSTUS
What art thou, the second?

COVETOUSNESS

I am Covetousness and might I have my wish, I would desire that this house and all the people in it were turned to gold, that I might lock you up in my good chest. O my sweet gold!

FAUSTUS

What art thou, the third?

WRATH

I am Wrath. I had neither father nor mother. I leaped out of a lion's mouth when I was scarce half an hour old. And ever since I have run up and down the world with this case of rapiers, wounding myself when I had nobody to fight withal. I was born in hell, and look to it, for some of you shall be my father.

FAUSTUS

What art thou, the fourth?

ENVY

I am Envy. I cannot read, and therefore wish all books were burnt. I am lean with seeing others eat. O, that there would come a famine through all the world, that all might die, and I live alone! Then thou shouldst see how fat I would be. But must thou sit and I stand? Come down, with a vengeance!

FAUSTUS

Away, envious rascal! What art thou, the fifth?

GLUTTONY

Who? I, sir? I am Gluttony. O, I come of a royal parentage. My grandfather was a gammon of bacon, my grandmother a hogshead of claret wine. Now, Faustus, thou hast heard all my progenitors, wilt thou bid me to supper?

FAUSTUS

No, I'll see thee hanged. Thou wilt eat up all my victuals.

GLUTTONY

Then the devil choke thee!

FAUSTUS

Choke thyself, glutton! What art thou, the sixth?

SLOTH

I am Sloth. I was begotten on a sunny bank, where I have lain ever since, and you have done me great injury to bring me from thence. Let me be carried thither again by Gluttony and Lechery. I'll not speak another word for a king's ransom.

FAUSTUS
What are you, Mistress Minx, the seventh and last?

LECHERY
Who I, sir? I am one that loves an inch of raw mutton better than an ell of fried stockfish, and the first letter of my name begins with lechery.

LUCIFER
Away, to hell, to hell!

Exit the SINS.

LUCIFER
Now, Faustus, how dost thou like this?

FAUSTUS
O, this feeds my soul!

LUCIFER
Tut, Faustus, in hell is all manner of delight.

FAUSTUS
O, might I see hell and return again, how happy were I then!

LUCIFER
Thou shalt. I will send for thee at midnight.
(Presenting a book.)
In meantime, take this book. Peruse it throughly, and thou shalt turn thyself into what shape thou wilt.

FAUSTUS
(Taking the book.)
Great thanks, mighty Lucifer. This will I keep as chary as my life.

LUCIFER
Farewell, Faustus, and think on the devil.

FAUSTUS
Farewell, great Lucifer. Come, Mephistopheles.

They exit.

SCENE 7

*The lights rise on a dressing room: a mirror ringed with lights, a
poster for 'Dr Faustus, Master of Concealed Arts, Paris', a costume
trunk covered in stickers, clothing rail. A rider of food and drink sits
on a table. Stage left a door to the shower and toilet, stage right a door
to corridor, stage and stage door.*

*WAGNER, in stage blacks and wearing a utility belt, headphones etc.
is eating a sandwich, drinking a Coke and reading a book.*

FAUSTUS
(Off, over tannoy.)
Great thanks, mighty Lucifer. This I will keep as chary as my life.

LUCIFER
(Over tannoy.)
Farewell, Faustus, and think on the devil.

STAGE MANAGEMENT
(Breaking in over tannoy.)
Stand by for interval…

*WAGNER reluctantly puts down her Coke and her magazine and
retrieves and prepares the suit of a stage conjuror.*

FAUSTUS
(Over tannoy.)
Farewell, great Lucifer. Come, Mephistopheles.

*Over the tannoy there is the whoosh and shebam of a stage bomb off, a
beat, then the eruption of applause.*

*Enter FAUSTUS from corridor, perspiring, make-up running, wired.
He is dressed as before and carries the book LUCIFER gave him. He
eats and consults his magic book for new tricks as WAGNER attempts
to change him from his previous costume into the conjuror's suit.*

WAGNER
Good house?

FAUSTUS
Slow.

WAGNER
I thought we'd sold out.

FAUSTUS
I did, in Wittenberg, weren't you listening?
(Laughs at his own joke.)
Packed to the rafters, they're just slow.

WAGNER
Seem to like you.

FAUSTUS
They love me, they fucking love me, Wagner.

FAUSTUS goes to plant a kiss on WAGNER.

WAGNER
(Swatting him away.)
Get off!

FAUSTUS
Now I'm a celebrity, I can misbehave.

WAGNER
Not with me you can't.

FAUSTUS half-dressed, playfully follows her around.

WAGNER
Get off, I said!

Enter MEPHISTOPHELES dressed as before.

In the course of the following MEPHISTOPHELES changes into the costume of a conjuror's assistant.

FAUSTUS
It's Mephistopheles I worry about.

WAGNER
Why?

FAUSTUS
She seems a bit down, morose, don't you think?
(Pointedly.)
Like she's stuck, in a dead-end job with twenty more years ahead of her, or a shit relationship she can't get out of.

MEPHISTOPHELES
Worry about yourself, Faustus, I am beyond your pity or your prayers.

FAUSTUS
But what have I to worry about?

FAUSTUS points a chicken leg stage left – a stage bomb. Plays a chord on an air guitar, a heavy metal chord is heard.

FAUSTUS
How does he do it, they ask, how does he do it?

MEPHISTOPHELES
Does he do it? They should be asking.

FAUSTUS doesn't rise to it. MEPHISTOPHELES turns FAUSTUS' chicken leg into a dildo as he is about to take a bite from it.

FAUSTUS
(To WAGNER.)
All the years of studying, all the hard work –

MEPHISTOPHELES
Wagner dear –

FAUSTUS
All the tedious old bastards I had to listen to, to respect –

MEPHISTOPHELES
Some tit-tape.

FAUSTUS
To hell with that!

MEPHISTOPHELES
Only I don't want a boob popping out.

FAUSTUS
To hell with all that, I said. Trier, Naples, Paris, everywhere I go, they love me. This is the life I dreamed of.

MEPHISTOPHELES
Consider it, how far the mind of man stretches! Barely to the end of his garden.

FAUSTUS inhales deeply, but is struck by something.

FAUSTUS
Wagner, have you changed shampoo recently?

WAGNER
(To FAUSTUS.)
Get off.

MEPHISTOPHELES
Wagner dear…

WAGNER
(To MEPHISTOPHELES.)
Yes.

FAUSTUS
There's something about you…

MEPHISTOPHELES
Tit-tape.

FAUSTUS
Something…

WAGNER
(To MEPHISTOPHELES.)
There's some in my bag. Under the props desk.

Exit WAGNER.

FAUSTUS
Long ago.

MEPHISTOPHELES
(Mimicking.)
Wagner, have you changed your shampoo recently? Only you smell like something, the milk of human kindness dripping from my mother's tit.

FAUSTUS
Are you jealous, Mephistopheles?

MEPHISTOPHELES
Of Wagner?

FAUSTUS
Her? Of me. Of my adoring public.

MEPHISTOPHELES

If such is the love you dream of, you're welcome to it.

FAUSTUS

What love do you dream of then, Mephistopheles?

MEPHISTOPHELES

Of that which is gone forever.

FAUSTUS

Surely there's always someone new. Especially in eternity.

MEPHISTOPHELES

Spare me another date with a soul in torment.

FAUSTUS

Well, you still have me and I am not in torment. For all you say that this is hell, if it is, it is a very tolerable hell.

MEPHISTOPHELES turns away.

FAUSTUS

They love me. They want to eat me up, my every word. Like you, they slaver in the hope of gobbling up my soul –

MEPHISTOPHELES

They might live in hope, I live in expectation.

FAUSTUS

I suppose it's not surprising you're jealous. Once Asiatic Emperors cowered under your sword, dead souls writhed under the wrath of Lucifer's right-hand man, now you totter about in fishnets, high heels and tit-tape, doing my bidding, while I get all the adulation. And the only limit to how far I go, is my imagination.

MEPHISTOPHELES

The world is safe then so.

FAUSTUS

You'll see how far my mind can stretch.

Enter WAGNER with tape which she hands to MEPHISTOPHELES.

WAGNER

Here.

MEPHISTOPHELES

You are a darling, Wagner.

WAGNER returns to helping FAUSTUS into his suit. FAUSTUS, when he thinks MEPHISTOPHELES is not looking and WAGNER is busy with pins etc. smells WAGNER's hair again.

MEPHISTOPHELES

Careful, Faustus, you have renounced love, remember, for the hot whore of celebrity.

FAUSTUS

Who said anything about love? To have is not to love, is it Wagner? You've loved and not had, haven't you?

WAGNER
(Distracted.)

I don't think I understand you, Dr Faustus.

MEPHISTOPHELES

Whereas you've been had and not been loved, Faustus.

FAUSTUS

And so I love to have, Mephistopheles. And I'll have and I'll have.

STAGE MANAGEMENT
(Over tannoy.)

Dr Faustus and Mephistopheles, to the stage please.

FAUSTUS

Now, my audience awaits me.

Exit FAUSTUS and MEPHISTOPHELES.

SCENE 8

The same dressing room. Nothing has changed except the poster which now reads 'Dr Faustus, Master of Concealed Arts, Rome'. There is a hubbub off. WAGNER is packing a trunk. At length the door opens and squeezing in through a throng of screaming people, FAUSTUS arrives. From the throng he pulls SAXON BRUNO, a fifty-something rockstar who in turn pulls on his twenty-something girlfriend ROBYN. They close the door to keep out the throng. FAUSTUS whoops and strikes his air guitar. Chords resound.

FAUSTUS
Sax the Axe! Sax the Axe!

They high five. FAUSTUS performs brief air guitar solo.

SAXON BRUNO
How do you do that, man?

ROBYN
It's like magic, real magic.

FAUSTUS
This is Wagner, Sax. Wagner, Saxon Bruno, the lead singer and axeman of Cursëd Necromancy.

FAUSTUS does an air guitar solo.

WAGNER
Cool. I mean hi –

SAXON BRUNO
Buenas babe, whatever.

Awkward beat.

SAXON BRUNO
And this is. . .what's this your name is babe?

ROBYN
Don't listen to him. He's only yanking my. . .you know.

ROBYN pulls imaginary chain and holds her nose, she is astonished to hear a real toilet flush.

ROBYN

You are just so magic! And that bit where you read my mind, it was like you could, I don't know, read my mind.

FAUSTUS

There's not much to it.

ROBYN laughs nervously.

ROBYN

I'm Robyn, only Sax's girlfriend.

FAUSTUS

How rude of me –

FAUSTUS goes to pass a beer to SAXON BRUNO.

SAXON BRUNO

Not like a pussy! Give the beast some air.

He throws SAXON BRUNO a beer. SAXON BRUNO shakes it violently then opens it. FAUSTUS follows suit. Beer explodes from the cans.

FAUSTUS

Yeah, like we give a shit.

The toilet door opens. Enter MEPHISTOPHELES.

ROBYN

O, so it wasn't…[a magical flush.]

MEPHISTOPHELES sits at her dressing table and quietly unmakes her face and changes.

FAUSTUS

Mephistopheles, this is Saxon Bruno.

SAXON BRUNO

Sax, please.

ROBYN

I thought you were very good too, Mrs Topheles.

SAXON BRUNO raises his shades to inspect MEPHISTOPHELES.

SAXON BRUNO

Say babe, weren't you backstage at Red Rocks in '77? The one where I bit the head off that live rat.

MEPHISTOPHELES
No. But I once sucked the eye out of a man and ate it in front of him.

SAXON BRUNO
Mescalin and speed can fuck you up.

MEPHISTOPHELES
You should try falling from the light of God.

SAXON BRUNO
Fuck God, the devil's got the best tunes.

FAUSTUS
Got to give him his due.

SAXON BRUNO
We've all had to stare the motherfucker in the eye on old Highway 61.

FAUSTUS
With you on that, man.

SAXON BRUNO
I meant us rockers. Dealing with the devil ain't no game for pussies. Pussies is for after the gig. Know what I mean?

MEPHISTOPHELES grabs his crotch squeezes it very tightly, then lets him go. He gasps.

MEPHISTOPHELES
Just wondering if you were all talk, or if there was something in those trousers.

SAXON BRUNO
(In pain, gasping.)
I like a chick with something between her legs.

MEPHISTOPHELES
I assure you, this chick has depths you could not hope to plumb, especially with that equipment.

SAXON BRUNO
(In pain, gasping.)
Well you going to show me or are you just a cockteaser?

ROBYN
Ahem, Sax. Please.

MEPHISTOPHELES
Yeah, stick to the ones who can tell the difference between a cock, and bull.

SAXON BRUNO
We should be going, babe.

ROBYN
So soon?

FAUSTUS
Please don't go –

SAXON BRUNO
Long and winding road back to the old *vecchio castello*. I'll leave you to your two clams, man, that one [Wagner], and the razor one [Mephistopheles]. But one thing, *hermano*, the reason I dropped by, we've got a tour coming up, and…

FAUSTUS
(Excited.)
Yes?

SAXON BRUNO
I was wondering whether you might be interested in, you know. . .

FAUSTUS
(Excited.)
Joining the band?

SAXON BRUNO
(Laughing/scoffing.)
You? Joining the Necros? What would you play? Fucking air guitar? I meant come do the special effects man.

FAUSTUS
The special effects?

ROBYN
Sax and the boys love illusions.

FAUSTUS
Illusions?

SAXON BRUNO
Yeah man, you could come be our pyro man. A few stage bombs, a few tricks.

FAUSTUS
Tricks?

SAXON BRUNO
Hey, what gives? It's an honour to be asked.

Beat.

FAUSTUS
You want to see a new trick?

SAXON BRUNO
Yeah, sure man. Why not?

FAUSTUS grabs ROBYN's crotch.

SAXON BRUNO
Hey man, hands off my taco.

FAUSTUS
It's all yours.

FAUSTUS grabs SAXON BRUNO's crotch.

SAXON BRUNO
Oi you fucking poof.

FAUSTUS releases them.

SAXON BRUNO
What the fuck? I've done better tricks with my dick.

FAUSTUS
Not any more.

ROBYN's dress rises.

ROBYN
O my God, Sax, O my God!

SAXON BRUNO
What the…?

SAXON BRUNO peeks into his jeans. He is aghast.

FAUSTUS

Maybe you need to hang with the pussies for a change.

ROBYN

O my God, Sax, what do I do? It's like I've no control over it.

Involuntarily ROBYN's new genitalia homes in on BRUNO's. He runs to escape her. FAUSTUS plays an air guitar solo. Eventually BRUNO escapes and exits. ROBYN follows. FAUSTUS has a moment of jubilation, and then is deflated.

FAUSTUS

They say you should never meet your heroes.

MEPHISTOPHELES

Is this not what you wanted?

FAUSTUS, to the accompaniment of the real sounds, smashes his air guitar in a temperamental outburst. Then watches WAGNER as she goes about her business.

FAUSTUS

Yes. No. I want something, something real, something tangible.

MEPHISTOPHELES waves her hand, a phone rings. WAGNER answers it.

FAUSTUS

Or else –

WAGNER passes phone to FAUSTUS who covers the mouthpiece and continues talking.

FAUSTUS

Why should I not just go back, back to my study, back to my books? To the way it was, Wagner and me?

(Answering phone.)

Dr John Faustus?

FAUSTUS listens with growing interest.

WAGNER
(Excited.)
Back to Wittenberg?

FAUSTUS
(Distracted.)
Yes.

WAGNER
I'll pack.

FAUSTUS
No.

WAGNER
Don't pack?

FAUSTUS
No, do pack. But not for Wittenberg.

WAGNER
Why?

FAUSTUS
Because this is it, Wagner, this is what I've been waiting for. The big break. Las Vegas.

He strikes an air guitar chord.

FAUSTUS
We're headlining the President's surprise birthday party.

MEPHISTOPHELES
What a disappointment man invariably turns out to be. Makes me long for Lucifer's ravening embrace.

FAUSTUS
O for once, Mephistopheles would you stop your moaning.

SCENE 9

A dressing room. The poster which reads 'Dr Faustus, Master of Concealed Arts, Las Vegas'. The rider has been cleared. A largely empty buffet table with sits in its place. A chaise longue downstage. FAUSTUS dressed in his sharpest suit yet reads his book, restlessly looking for a new trick. Enter WAGNER who crosses with trays of canapés which she places on the buffet table. Exit WAGNER. Enter WAGNER with bottles of champagne, she places them down on the table. Exit WAGNER. FAUSTUS tries not to be distracted by her, but he cannot help himself. Before she returns, he sneaks one of the canapés. Then another. He is just about to eat a third when enter WAGNER with a tray of glasses.

WAGNER
There's a line of limos out there. The special guests are arriving.

WAGNER sees the canapé. FAUSTUS puts the canapé down and smiles guiltily. She smacks his hand.

WAGNER
Some day I'll have to take you in hand.

FAUSTUS
(Smiling.)
Why someday?

An awkward beat.

WAGNER
It's just a saying.

They both revert to what they were doing.

FAUSTUS
If you could do anything by magic, Wagner, what would it be?

WAGNER
I can't do magic.

FAUSTUS
But if you could, would you use it to do something big, something good? Like wars, or hunger?

WAGNER

If something like that were possible, someone would have tried it long ago.

FAUSTUS

Maybe there hasn't been someone with my powers.

WAGNER

Yeah, sure. Dream on!
(Thinking as she works.)
But even if you could fix something by magic, like wars or hunger, they wouldn't stay fixed. You'd have to fix people. And to fix them you'd have to fix their abilities to fuck things up. Which is sort of what makes us human.

WAGNER smacks FAUSTUS' hand as he reaches for another canapé.

FAUSTUS

But if I had real magic?

WAGNER

In which case, you'd be, like, God? In which case, what would you be waiting for? The world is full of people trying to be God, or thinking they're God. The best we can do is try to be decent to those around us, and then maybe if the next person does that, and the next… Maybe then.

WAGNER goes to lift a crate of glasses.

FAUSTUS

Let me.

FAUSTUS attempts to take them from her.

WAGNER

(Not unaffectionate.)
Get off! You've got a show to do and I've got a million and one things to sort for the afters.

Beat.

FAUSTUS

(Risking it, serious.)
Do you like me, Wagner?

WAGNER for the briefest moment stops what she's doing, then starts again.

WAGNER
(Attempted nonchalance.)
What kind of a question's that?

FAUSTUS
You know.

Beat.

WAGNER
Yeah, sure. But lots of people like you. You're famous, remember.

WAGNER starts to fold napkins. FAUSTUS goes to help her, by copying what she's doing, unsuccessfully.

FAUSTUS
But as a person, do you like me as a person?

WAGNER
You seem happier with many people liking you.

FAUSTUS
You think I'm shallow?

WAGNER
I didn't say that. Some people want to be loved by many. Others just want to love one person, and be loved by one person in return. The first are called celebrities, the second…losers, I suppose.

Awkward beat. FAUSTUS looks for something to say.

FAUSTUS
What's your first name, Wagner? You never told me.

WAGNER
Grace.

FAUSTUS
Grace. Call me John, Grace.

Beat.

WAGNER
(Significantly.)
Sometimes, though, what people want, it can change. If they're willing –

Enter MEPHISTOPHELES. She is dressed for the show. She busies herself, making up, going and returning to the bathroom, but always keeping an ear out for their conversation.

FAUSTUS
(Sotto.)
Why should I want to change, when I have everything I want?

WAGNER
(Sotto, bitter.)
And you've got her and she's got you.

FAUSTUS
(Sotto.)
You don't like her?

WAGNER
(Sotto, wary.)
Something not quite right about her. Like under the surface there's nothing there. Just a void. An emptiness.

FAUSTUS
(Sotto.)
It is purely a business arrangement, if that is what you are thinking.

WAGNER
(Sotto.)
It's none of my business, Dr Faustus.

FAUSTUS
(Sotto.)
Maybe I can change, Grace, maybe I can –

MEPHISTOPHELES vomits into one of FAUSTUS' shoes.

WAGNER
O my goodness! Are you okay?

MEPHISTOPHELES
Something just got stuck in my craw.

STAGE MANAGEMENT
(Over tannoy.)
Guests entering the auditorium. Curtain in five.

WAGNER
I'll get you some soda water.

MEPHISTOPHELES
You are a dear.

WAGNER takes off her apron and exits.

MEPHISTOPHELES
(Under her breath.)
Like Bambi's mother.

FAUSTUS consults his book with renewed interest. He takes notes.
MEPHISTOPHELES regards him. He stops.

FAUSTUS
I think you *are* jealous!

MEPHISTOPHELES bursts out laughing.

MEPHISTOPHELES
Of you?
(Laughing.)
Of her? Are you forgetting, that I was once a man, and that
as a man I knew love, a love that makes your skin-crawling
stammerings of dumb affection the potato prints of a child upon
the nursery wall.

FAUSTUS
You were once in love?

MEPHISTOPHELES
I loved. It was a garden. Walled. Secret. Cooled by streams and
fountains. And I lost it. And after, I burned the garden to the
ground. And the village, the town, the city. I burned and I burned.
What is love? Enough of love. Burn love. The world awaits you.
Forget her, forget Wagner.

STAGE MANAGEMENT
(Over tannoy.)
Three minutes to curtain.

FAUSTUS
She's called Grace.

MEPHISTOPHELES
Forget Grace.

FAUSTUS
Why should I?

MEPHISTOPHELES
Why her when you could have any woman you want? She is so common or garden, so nothing. And in time she will come to seem so nothing to you. How many years have passed since we struck our bargain?

FAUSTUS
Some. A few.

MEPHISTOPHELES
But those that have passed now seem briefer than a dream?

FAUSTUS shrugs, reluctant to admit it.

MEPHISTOPHELES
And when all twenty-four have gone, will your life then not seem shorter than a day? Will you want to be able to say that this…this lackey, this skivvy –

FAUSTUS
She's not, she's my student. She was my student.

MEPHISTOPHELES
Will that husk of a memory keep you warm for eternity?

STAGE MANAGEMENT
(Over tannoy.)
Orchestra. Dancers. Stand by for curtain.

MEPHISTOPHELES
Listen, the village, the town, the city is out there for the taking. Fame or infamy, it doesn't matter, they are the only immortality

available to man. To sin big is to rise above the mediocrity of the masses. Sin big. Sin famously.

STAGE MANAGEMENT
(Over tannoy.)
Dr Faustus, Mephistopheles to the stage please.

MEPHISTOPHELES
Time to light those flames.

FAUSTUS nods. MEPHISTOPHELES opens the door.

FAUSTUS
I'll be with you in a minute.

FAUSTUS goes to his book. He consults something. He takes out a notebook and scribbles one last note and puts the slip of paper in his pocket. He is about to go when he sees WAGNER's apron. He conjures a flower and places it on the apron. Exit FAUSTUS.

MC
(Over tannoy.)
And now please put your hands together for the world famous master of concealed arts, Dr John Faustus.

The scene continues to:

SCENE 10

A montage of scenes.

WAGNER returns with a soda. As the introductory music strikes up over the tannoy, she realises she is too late. She sits on the chaise longue. The introductory music comes to an end. She sips the soda.

FAUSTUS
(Over tannoy.)
Mr President, your Highness, Holy Father, distinguished ladies and gentlemen, welcome to my humble show –

Over the tannoy a crash of Cursëd Necromancy cords evolves into the 'Star Spangled Banner' to great applause. WAGNER is about to open her book when she sees the flower.

Cross fade to:

WAGNER now holds the flower and listens tensely.

FAUSTUS
(Over tannoy.)
Now, look in your breast pockets, Gentlemen. . .cheques for millions of pounds. Made out to? Save the Children, Save the Animals and Save the Planet. Please give our banker, media mogul and politician friends a big round of applause.

Applause.

Cross fade to:

The dressing room is empty, WAGNER enters, with yet more plates of canapés, and drinks etc. The flower is now in a vase. She stops and listens.

FAUSTUS
(Over tannoy.)
Bell, book and candle, candle book and bell,
Holy Father, damn all these sinning priests to hell.

POPE
(Over tannoy.)
In nomine patris, filii, spiritus sancti in perpetuo ad infernum damno.

Astonishment is heard over the tannoy, wild applause.

WAGNER is impressed.

Cross fade to:

WAGNER is wrestling with a champagne bottle cork, but intent upon the show.

FAUSTUS
(Over tannoy.)
And now, specially for you, from the grave, Mr President, your predecessor, President Abraham Lincoln.

Gasps. The cork pops out to WAGNER's surprise.

FAUSTUS
(Over tannoy.)
Don't be afraid. Go to him. Check him out. Tug his beard.

Applause.

Cross fade to:

ABRAHAM LINCOLN
(Over tannoy.)
Fellow Citizens, we cannot escape history. No personal significance or insignificance can spare one or another of us. The fiery trial through which we pass will light us down in honour or dishonour to the last generation.

Applause. Huge applause. WAGNER is really impressed.

Cross fade to:

FAUSTUS
(Over tannoy.)
Thank you, thank you, Mr President, illustrious guests. My name is Dr John Faustus –

STAGE MANAGEMENT
(Over tannoy.)
Standby for interval, curtain in five, four –

FAUSTUS
And don't you be going away, there's still much more to come.

STAGE MANAGEMENT
(Over tannoy.)
Two, and one.

Applause.

STAGE MANAGEMENT
(Over tannoy.)
Everyone take fifteen.

To dark.

Interval.

SCENE 11

A thronged party is in full swing in the narrow confines of FAUSTUS'
dressing room. Guests are high spirited and throb in dance as one
beast. Amidst the throng are the POPE, the QUEEN, a MINISTER,
a BANKER, a MEDIA MOGUL, MEPHISTOPHELES with FAUSTUS
at the centre of it. Through the throbbing throng WAGNER struggles
valiantly with plates of canapés and trays of champagne. FAUSTUS
escapes momentarily as WAGNER goes for fresh supplies.

FAUSTUS
What did you think of the show, Grace?

WAGNER
Not bad.

FAUSTUS
So you thought it was good?

WAGNER gives FAUSTUS a peck on the cheek. She blushes. FAUSTUS
smiles and takes the last glass of champagne from her tray and returns
to the throng.

BANKER and MEPHISTOPHELES above the throng.

BANKER
Don't I know you from someplace?

MEPHISTOPHELES
What was it you said you did?

BANKER
Banking.

MEPHISTOPHELES
Yes, you know me.

BANKER
Say, that cheque the conjuror had me hand over.

MEPHISTOPHELES
What about it?

BANKER
I took a lot of trouble to avoid that tax, I'm not handing it over to
some charity.

MEPHISTOPHELES

If you care to sign this contract, I'll be happy to return your cheque to you.

MEPHISTOPHELES produces a contract. The BANKER reads.

MEDIA MOGUL

Hi there, I'll have my cheque back too, if you don't mind.

MEPHISTOPHELES

And you are?

MEDIA MOGUL

I am a media mogul. And I didn't spend my life building an empire to give it away to poor people.

MEPHISTOPHELES hands the MEDIA MOGUL a contract.

MINISTER

Hello, I'm Chancellor of the Exchequer, I couldn't help but overhear but that money wasn't really mine to give away –

MEPHISTOPHELES conjures a third contract.

BANKER

What's all this about the soul?

MEPHISTOPHELES

Only applicable in the event you have one.

BANKER, MEDIA MOGUL and MINISTER are relieved. They frisk themselves for pens.

MEPHISTOPHELES cuts open their arms as she did FAUSTUS' earlier. They sign their contracts in blood.

MEPHISTOPHELES

Gentlemen, your cheques.

It rains down a confetti of cheques. The BANKER, MINISTER and MEDIA MOGUL are delighted. They are once more drawn back into the throng. FAUSTUS has caught a piece of the confetti.

FAUSTUS
What's this, Mephistopheles? The money I made them give to charity.

MEPHISTOPHELES
A piece of advice, Faustus, if you want to play with the big boys, don't piss them off. If you piss them off, you'll only get to do it once, then they'll bury you and forget you. This way, you can continue to play with them.

FAUSTUS
(Referring to contracts.)
But what are these?

MEPHISTOPHELES
Just a little side business. They were only too happy to sign, so little did they value their souls. They'll be eating shit from the devil's arsehole for eternity.

FAUSTUS
(Worried.)
What about me?

MEPHISTOPHELES
You are worth so much more.

FAUSTUS
I am?

MEPHISTOPHELES
Because you value your soul. Just as I did mine.

FAUSTUS
So I won't have to eat shit?

MEPHISTOPHELES
No.
(She smiles)
You'll long to eat shit.

The music rises, the dancing takes over. MEPHISTOPHELES returns into the throng.

The POPE having spotted FAUSTUS' book on the chaise longue, goes to inspect it.

FAUSTUS deeply troubled, takes another glass of wine and goes to him. The POPE strokes the book.

POPE
I have long been a fan of conjuring.

FAUSTUS
Bread into flesh, water into wine and all that?

POPE
How it might appear to those of little faith. But you strike me Dr Faustus as a man of some faith.

FAUSTUS
Faith in what? That is the question.

POPE
In the existence of the Lord, Our Saviour.

The POPE, has hit a nerve, he smiles.

POPE
Since, as a man of learning you must accept, that to believe in the antithesis, one must believe in the thesis itself. That is why they say Lucifer is so sulky, since to revolt against God is to acknowledge his existence.
(Chuckling.)
Every time Lucifer destroys something, he acknowledges God's creation.

WAGNER comes round with some canapés.

POPE
Ah, black truffles with caviar. A fine creation. Black on black, one might say. But what is black? Is there such a thing as pure, sightless black? Or is there always some light, some contour to the dark that offers hope? Evil is so very interesting, don't you think? Since it gains its existence only from mankind's abjuration of good, it is itself a product of God's goodness. But you know this, of course.

FAUSTUS does not respond.

Even in the darkest night, you can only perceive the dark thanks to the light of our Lord. That trick where you had me damn those priests to hell, I've read of this trick before. We have this book in the Sistine Library you see. It was obtained by one of my more wayward predecessors in the Middle Ages.

FAUSTUS
It wasn't a trick, I punished the hypocrisy of those who claim to be good.

POPE
The only magic in the world is that of God's creation. The rest is showmanship. All the devil was ever good for. His tricks are as nothing. He longs for there to be nothing. But creation keeps confounding him.

FAUSTUS struggles with himself.

FAUSTUS
Sometimes I think of hell, of how long eternity is, and I despair, Holy Father.

MEPHISTOPHELES
(Approaching.)
I'm afraid Dr Faustus must be going, the President –

POPE
To despair is hell, Faustus, that is what you must guard against. The hell within. To despair is the greatest sin. And you will be damned to play out your despair night after night, for eternity. Hope is the light. Remember the light.

The POPE stands and smiles. He strokes MEPHISTOPHELES' cheek.

POPE
Mephistopheles, such an evocative name.

MEPHISTOPHELES
Nothing would give me greater pleasure than to entertain you, Holy Father.

POPE
I'm sorry, I must forego such undoubted pleasures. While the Church of Rome is unchanging and eternal, we have, over time been forced to mend some of our more indulgent indulgences.

The POPE rejoins the throng. FAUSTUS regards MEPHISTOPHELES balefully.

MEPHISTOPHELES hands FAUSTUS another glass of champagne and leads him back into the throng.

MEPHISTOPHELES turns up an imaginary dial. The noise and the temperature rise. The beat transforms into 'Hail to the Chief'. Enter two SECRET SERVICEMEN who check the place and guests. They are followed by the PRESIDENT. The throng parts in front of him. FAUSTUS stands out to welcome him. He is swaying slightly.

FAUSTUS
Mr President, I would just like to say, on behalf of everyone here, what an honour it is for me, I mean to be able to perform for you on your birthday, I mean for us to be able to celebrate your birthday with you.

Ripple of applause.

PRESIDENT
Thank you, Dr Faustus, and I'm sorry I was late but I was in conference with my predecessor President Lincoln, who you so kindly conjured from the dead for me. Most illuminating to have his thoughts on the current state of the union. I am in your debt.

FAUSTUS
(Bowing deeply.)
It really was nothing, Mr President. Now, I hope you don't mind, but I've arranged a little entertainment, for your birthday.

PRESIDENT
Really, you've done enough already –

FAUSTUS claps his hands. The room goes silent. FAUSTUS nods to MEPHISTOPHELES.

FAUSTUS
Because, what do you get for the man who has everything?

FAUSTUS plays an air guitar chord and launches into an elaborate intro to 'Happy Birthday'. The lights dim. MEPHISTOPHELES conjures MARILYN MONROE who sings 'Happy Birthday' for the PRESIDENT. She sings it seductively and drapes herself over the

PRESIDENT. Eventually the PRESIDENT succumbs and they kiss. FAUSTUS continues playing, wilder and wilder, even as the lights return and the PRESIDENT and the other guests realise he is kissing a devil. There is much screaming and mayhem. The SECRET SERVICE MEN attempt to protect the PRESIDENT and facilitate his escape, but the door is blocked by another devil dressed as ABRAHAM LINCOLN. Much screaming and mayhem as FAUSTUS continues to play. At length, as FAUSTUS finishes his solo, the room is cleared.

FAUSTUS
Mr President? Mr President? Where is everyone?

SCENE 12

Later. WAGNER tidies the detritus of the party. FAUSTUS is deflated and still semi-drunk. He stands on his own. Eating a tray of canapés. He stops.

FAUSTUS

Stupid. Stupid, stupid, stupid, stupid. For all your brains, what a stupid ass you are, Faustus, trying to win the approval of the world with tricks and trifles.

He considers the canapé and discards it in disgust. WAGNER looks on disapprovingly.

FAUSTUS

I am stuffed –

FAUSTUS takes an empty champagne bottle from the tray WAGNER carries.

FAUSTUS

I am stuffed with –

He tips the bottle. Nothing.

FAUSTUS

Nothing. Nothingness. No amount of stuff can fill it up.

WAGNER

Go back to the hotel. Sleep it off.

WAGNER takes the bottle.

FAUSTUS

Grace?

WAGNER

Yes?

FAUSTUS is awkward, does not know how to declare himself. He conjures from nowhere a diamond necklace.

WAGNER

They must belong to Mephistopheles.

FAUSTUS

No. No, they're for you.

WAGNER
But why?

FAUSTUS
Because…because you inspired me. Because you make me think I could be better than I am.

WAGNER
I did nothing. I just made the canapés.

FAUSTUS
No. No. I am nothing. Nothing-ness. A pit of nothing-ness.

WAGNER
Jesus wept!

FAUSTUS
But he did not weep for me.

WAGNER
Christ! It's a saying. Go back to the hotel, sleep it off. In the morning maybe they'll have forgotten. Hopefully. And we'll be some place else. Hopefully.

FAUSTUS
Grace?

WAGNER
What?

FAUSTUS smells her hair. WAGNER smiles but then tries to pull away. FAUSTUS tries to kiss her. She pushes him off.

WAGNER
No. What are you doing?

FAUSTUS
Why not? I'm a bad man. This is what bad men do.

FAUSTUS makes another half-hearted attempt.

WAGNER
No, stop it. Stop. Not here. Not like this. You need to sober up. You need to get away from all this. It's messing with your head. You need to get away from her.

FAUSTUS

You're afraid? Afraid Mephistopheles might discover us? To hell
with Mephistopheles.
  (Laughs, bitter.)
To hell with Mephistopheles.

WAGNER

Who cares about Mephistopheles!

FAUSTUS

No one cares for Mephistopheles, except the Devil, and –
  (Tapping his nose.)
Frankly I think they're in some kind of abusive relationship
together.

WAGNER

What is it she holds over you?

FAUSTUS

Something she would hold over you if I told you.

FAUSTUS attempts to kiss her again.

WAGNER

Later. When you've sobered up. When she's not around.

*Enter MEPHISTOPHELES. FAUSTUS presses the diamonds on
WAGNER.*

FAUSTUS

Ah Mephistopheles, still here?

MEPHISTOPHELES

The devil never sleeps.

FAUSTUS

Not like us mortals.

MEPHISTOPHELES

Though I feel a weariness no mortal could imagine.

FAUSTUS

Because you must watch my every move?

MEPHISTOPHELES

And how tedious those moves are.

FAUSTUS
(Feigning tiredness.)
I'm going back to the hotel. I'll see you both later.

MEPHISTOPHELES
Not if I see you first.

MEPHISTOPHELES smiles. Exit FAUSTUS. WAGNER continues to work, MEPHISTOPHELES looks at her.

MEPHISTOPHELES
You know I wasn't always like this, Wagner, a void, wasn't it? Nothing under the surface?

WAGNER
You heard?

MEPHISTOPHELES smiles.

MEPHISTOPHELES
I was once in love too.

WAGNER
(Shrugging.)
Who's in love?

MEPHISTOPHELES
She was like you, shy, but she was beautiful.

WAGNER goes to leave, MEPHISTOPHELES stays her.

MEPHISTOPHELES
I was different then. And she was the flower of femininity, graceful, yet with so little thought of herself and so much of others, that she thought herself undeserving of me. Like you she was happy to live her life in the shadows. She lived with her parents, in a high walled house in the countryside. I can still see her walking in her garden. Her face was unknown at Court, and I was happy to keep it so. But one day when I was riding with the Emperor – I was one of his favourites – some of the other royal young men were boasting, saying their girls were this or that. And the Emperor turned to me and said, what about you, Mephisto, do you not have a girl that compares? As I said, I was young, and boastful. And I said that my love surpassed all others, in beauty, grace and spirit. The Emperor said then we must settle this and

all men must bring their mistresses to Court. And I, too proud to back down and save myself and my love, took her to Court. And the Emperor agreed that my love was the most lovely. In fact he fell for her himself and demanded that he have her himself. I refused. But he offered me honours, powers, dominions. And the more I refused, the more he offered. And I was young and ambitious. And in the end I said she's yours.

Beat.

WAGNER
This is a fairytale. I've heard it before.

MEPHISTOPHELES
It is a fairy tale that was first told about me. But they changed the ending.

WAGNER
How did it end?

MEPHISTOPHELES
The Emperor had her, and soon tired of her. After, I'd have nothing to do with her. I had made my decision. She killed herself. And I took up my new honours, powers and dominions and I burnt and raped and robbed my way though the Empire until I reached the gates of the palace. And the Emperor himself pleaded for mercy at my feet. I nailed him to a tree, cut him open, and let the birds eat him alive.

WAGNER
I must be going.

MEPHISTOPHELES stops her.

MEPHISTOPHELES
So soon?

WAGNER
Yes.

MEPHISTOPHELES takes her firmly by the hands. At first WAGNER attempts to resist.

MEPHISTOPHELES
I think we should get to know each other a little better. There's so much we could share with each other.

Exit MEPHISTOPHELES leading WAGNER off.

SCENE 13

The dressing room is in moonlit darkness. It is near midnight but otherwise as before. The door opens. Enter SECRET SERVICE MAN. He checks the coast is clear. He signals for a full SWAT TEAM to enter. Methodically the SWAT TEAM go through FAUSTUS' things. In the trunk they find Faustus'/Lucifer's book. SECRET SERVICE MAN reads it with disgust. He bags the book. Off he hears someone coming. He signals his men to exit via the bathroom, turns off the light. They are gone just as –

SCENE 14

– the door opens, enter FAUSTUS sobered, dressed in his casual best clothes. He conjures a bunch of flowers and a vase. He tries the vase out in various positions. He then checks his watch and attempts a relaxed position, but he is too agitated. He sits on the edge of the chaise longue. Pause. The SECRET SERVICE MAN and SWAT TEAM are about to pounce when – the door opens. Enter WAGNER dressed in high heels and a raincoat, gloves and a headscarf. FAUSTUS is amazed by the transformation and holds out his arms to her. WAGNER walks towards FAUSTUS, takes off her gloves and her headscarf and drapes them over FAUSTUS' outstretched arms.

Confused at her change in manner, FAUSTUS rushes to fix her a drink. WAGNER takes off her raincoat, throws it over FAUSTUS' arm as he hands her the drink. To FAUSTUS' great surprise WAGNER wears only stylish underwear.

WAGNER downs the drink in one then leads FAUSTUS to the sofa.

WAGNER gets down on her knees and starts to undress FAUSTUS from the shoes up as he talks.

FAUSTUS

Wagner. Grace. Before we, you know, I want you to know that I am aware I probably haven't always expressed my appreciation of you, your kindnesses, your generosity. But I am aware that you've always been there for me. Because, Grace, because – look at me, please –

Beat. WAGNER finishes by removing FAUSTUS' shirt. He stands in his boxer shorts. She pushes him to the sofa and straddles him. There is much grunting and grinding. Smoke begins to emanate from the sofa.

The SECRET SERVICE MAN and his SWAT TEAM peep out from behind the door of the bathroom. They take photos.

Building to a first climax the sofa tips over backwards and FAUSTUS and WAGNER disappear behind it. All we now see are hands, feet, buttocks and other body parts while the grunting and climaxing intensifies. Soon other objects begin to appear in the hands that we see – handcuffs, a pump, a circular saw etc. We can judge what is going on by the horror, disgust and confusion on the faces of the SECRET

*SERVICE MAN and SWAT team. It becomes so appalling that the
SECRET SERVICE MAN won't let the SWAT TEAM look. As the hidden
sexual activity reaches its climax, the SECRET SERVICE MAN decides
he's got to put a stop to it. Once again he is just about to emerge from
the hiding place when –*

*– the door opens and enter WAGNER, tied, gagged and cuffed. She is
dressed as before. The SECRET SERVICE MAN and the SWAT TEAM
quickly retreat to the bathroom. WAGNER hops over to the light switch
and with her forehead hits it.*

*Everything goes quiet and still. Slowly, from behind the sofa FAUSTUS
crawls, he is begrimed, bloody, burnt, beaten. He too wears handcuffs,
he has a gimp ball in his mouth. He stops when he sees WAGNER. He
looks back to the sofa. He spits the ball out of his mouth. He pushes
the sofa out of the way, and there behind it is MEPHISTOPHELES,
immaculate, dressed in the same underwear she wore as Wagner.*

MEPHISTOPHELES

Hope you didn't mind me borrowing your body, dear. Well you
don't think I was going to put mine through all that? And with
him? Don't worry, it will only hurt badly for a while. But there
again, what are the agonies of the body compared to the torments
of the immortal soul? Time you went back to Wittenberg. As you
can see, I can satisfy his needs from here on in.

*MEPHISTOPHELES goes towards the door. WAGNER looks to
FAUSTUS. Pause.*

FAUSTUS

We'll both go back to Wittenberg. I'll return to my researches. That
will be enough for us. We'll live out quietly the rest of our days.

MEPHISTOPHELES

You only have ten years.

FAUSTUS

So? I will know love for ten years.

MEPHISTOPHELES

You'll be lucky if love lasts the one. The same face, the same body,
day-in-day-out, night-in-night-out? And when the kids come?
Mewling, pissing, puking. You'll soon begin to miss the old magic.

Remember your parents. What love there was died long before the crash. Love is a crash. One minute you're flying though the air, the next you are all over the road in pieces. Get rid of her, Faustus, send her back.

FAUSTUS
But you knew love. The girl? The garden?

MEPHISTOPHELES
No. I discovered the lie of love. And I hated God for what he did to me. Just as you Faustus hated him for taking away your parents. We hated him that his creation could cause such pain. And that our pain was part of his creation. Send her back, Faustus.

FAUSTUS
But without pain there would be no free will, we would all be bound to be good.

MEPHISTOPHELES
What free will? Man is bound. Don't you see? God's creation is grandest illusion, a spectacle full of light and sound and beauty, which man thinks he moves through at his own free will. But he is just a player in that spectacle. And to love, to procreate is to perpetuate the show, to play along with the whole charade. To play along with the Grand Illusionist. The only power, the only freedom, the only real autonomy man can have is to destroy. To destroy what God has created. Destroy it, Faustus, destroy love. Send her back.

FAUSTUS
But what of redemption? What of salvation?

MEPHISTOPHELES
For some perhaps it might be possible, Faustus, but not for you. You stood up to him, Faustus, so he hates you. God hates you. Send her back.

Pause. FAUSTUS sits. He is in despair. WAGNER goes to him.

WAGNER
No John. It's not true.

Pause.

FAUSTUS
It is. Go.

WAGNER
Please.

FAUSTUS
She's right. I cannot go back. I have forfeited, by my own free will, the right to happiness, love, and to be loved. I see that now. Go.

WAGNER
No. You haven't. You are loved. You are not a bad person. Your show tonight, the money for charity.

FAUSTUS
Tricks. Nothing more than empty tricks. To impress you. Now go before it is too late for you. Or you will be as loathsome to yourself as I am to me.

FAUSTUS pushes her towards the door.

WAGNER
I'll go. She's right, but only about one thing. The agonies of the body are bearable, but those of the soul…

FAUSTUS does not turn. WAGNER slips out of the room.

MEPHISTOPHELES
(Throwing him a towel.)
Clean yourself up, Faustus, you're a mess.

MEPHISTOPHELES tightens her belt and exits.

FAUSTUS looks at himself. He is indeed filthy and largely naked. He feels very small. He looks to the heavens, shivers and puts on the dressing gown. Exit FAUSTUS to shower. As he showers the SECRET SERVICE MEN ready themselves to ambush him on his return. Enter the showered FAUSTUS. He dries his hair.

FAUSTUS
The time draws near and I feel the cold hand of despair slide around my throat. No. Do not despair, they say, one of the thieves was saved. But that was the other one, not me. Not me. Grace? She's gone. She could not have saved you. Nothing can. Now there's only sleep. Let the remaining years pass in a dream. In sleep.

He sits down wearily.

SCENE 15

FAUSTUS looks up to find the SECRET SERVICE MEN and the SWAT TEAM with all guns trained on him.

FAUSTUS

What? Have you come for me so soon? But my time is not yet run.

SECRET SERVICE MAN shakes his head, then slugs FAUSTUS in the stomach and signals to his colleagues who approach FAUSTUS, cuff him and cover his head with a sack. To the SECRET SERVICE MAN's astonishment the sacked head comes off and FAUSTUS' headless body collapses to the floor.

SECRET SERVICE MAN

What the fuck?

Enter MEPHISTOPHELEs, they freeze.

MEPHISTOPHELES

Why don't I give you a hand with that?

A SWAT TEAM member leaps back in horror from the body.

SECRET SERVICE MAN

Hold your position.

SWAT TEAM MEMBER

But he's alive again.

SECRET SERVICE MAN

Give him his head!

The headless body takes the sacked head in its hands. The head speaks.

FAUSTUS

Keep it, I'll have heads and hands and all your stinking hearts, to pay you back for this. You want to know who I work for? I work for the devil, and the devil works for me. We have a deal and our deal still has some years to run, so even if you'd cut me into a million tiny pieces, as small as desert sand you still have up your assholes from Iraq and Afghanistan, I'd have come back unharmed to fuck you up. Mephistopheles, go take these men on your burning back, up to the height of heaven, then toss them down into the lowest hell. No, that way the world won't see their shame, or know the power of Faustus. No, drag them first across the deserts, plains and cities of the world, till all their bones are broken and dismembered, as they wanted mine to be, but keep them alive, so they can say who did this to them.

SECRET SERVICE MAN
Jesus, pity us, Dr Faustus, for the love of God –

FAUSTUS

Fuck God. I'm done with pity, I'm done with love. I'm done with hope.

Exit MEPHISTOPHELES and DEVILS with the SECRET SERVICE MAN and the SWAT TEAM.

SCENE 16

A montage of scenes.

As the sound of the SECRET SERVICE MAN and SWAT TEAM being tormented continues, FAUSTUS sits glumly alone in his dressing room. He eats disinterestedly. Enter a THEATRE MANAGER. He is shocked at the state of the room. He calls a team of STAGE HANDS. The STAGE HANDS tidy the room. They finish by removing his gold sofa.

Cross fade to:

FAUSTUS eats. The dressing room is the same only smaller. Maybe more items have disappeared. The poster on the wall now has another celebrated contemporary magician's name at the top, Faustus is reduced to a supporting role.

LUCIFER
(Off, over tannoy.)
I will send for thee at midnight. In meantime, take this book. Peruse it throughly, and thou shalt turn thyself into what shape thou wilt.

MAGICIAN
(Off, over tannoy.)
Great thanks, mighty Lucifer. This will I keep as chary as my life.

LUCIFER
(Off, over tannoy.)
Farewell, [Magician's name], and think on the devil.

MAGICIAN
(Off, over tannoy.)
Farewell, great Lucifer. Come, Beelzebub.

The cities scroll by. 'Ibiza, Ayia Napa, EuroDisney, Leeds, Glasgow, Trier' FAUSTUS sits as before only fatter.

Enter MEPHISTOPHELES. She is unimpressed by the new dressing room.

MC
(Over tannoy.)
They say you only play Trier Peoples Theatre twice in your
career, once on the way up and once on the way down. So put
your hands together and welcome back Dr John Faustus.

There's a smattering of applause. Wearily FAUSTUS gets up and exits.

Cross fade to:

*MEPHISTOPHELES sits in the dressing room. She files her nails and
reads 'Hello'. There's a knock at the door. Onstage the celebrated
contemporary magician is heard over the tannoy.*

MAGICIAN
(Over tannoy.)
And now, specially for you, from the grave, Mr President, Dr
Martin Luther King.

*Huge applause. FAUSTUS shakes his head, the MAGICIAN has stolen
his trick and has gone one better.*

Gasps.

MAGICIAN
(Over tannoy.)
Don't be afraid. Go to him. Check him out.

Applause.

Cross fade to:

MARTIN LUTHER KING
(Over tannoy.)
I am happy to join with you today in what will go down in history
as the greatest demonstration for freedom in the history of our
nation.

Applause. Huge applause.

*The THEATRE MANAGER enters. The toilet flushes. FAUSTUS emerges,
hair greyer, fatter. The THEATRE MANAGER shakes his head, hands
FAUSTUS an envelope and points towards the door. The STAGE
HANDS enter and start removing much of what little remains while
the celebrated contemporary magician plays on.*

MAGICIAN

(Over tannoy.)

My name is [Magician's name]. And don't you be going away, there's still much more to come.

Applause off.

STAGE MANAGEMENT

(Over tannoy.)

And cue music.

SCENE 17

'The Birdy Song' or 'Agadoo' and a small audience clapping along plays over the tannoy as lights rise on a tiny, dirty, litter-strewn, end-of-pier dressing room. A tatty poster with 'All You Can Eat Stars of Yesteryear Balti Evening at the Rhode Palladium'.

FAUSTUS now old, tired and overweight, sits listlessly eating a slice of pizza while MEPHISTOPHELES helps him out of his now faded, shabby suit. Similarly MEPHISTOPHELES, while the same age as ever, wears a tatty version of her previous clothes. She hangs up the jacket and turns off the tannoy and sits and files her nails.

A couple, fans, stand watching them awkwardly.

DUCHESS

Well I liked it. I really did. The illusions. The tricks. So good they were almost real. That bit where you pretended to kill all those CIA agents. Or were they FBI? One of them plays at home and one of them plays away?

(She laughs.)

I can never remember which. Truth be told, I wasn't sure where you were meant to be at that point. Was it still Las Vegas or had you moved on? It got a bit confusing. And the way the years raced by, so it seemed only a short time since you made the deal with him-whose-name-we-dare-not-say and then you were saying your time was up. Sad really. But I suppose it makes you think. But it was still a good show. They always have the best here at the 'All You Can Eat Monday's Stars of Yesteryear Balti Evening in Rhode'. But that was the thing, no matter how much I ate tonight I just couldn't fill up. It was like I had a hole in me…

(Holds her pregnant stomach.)

…or Junior had. And then when your friend the Pope mentioned the black truffle with caviar, I got this sudden hunger, and I thought that's what I want, that's what I need, that's what I've got to have. Black, black foods, dribbling down my throat, feeding him, my baby. And I says to Duke…

(Puts a hand on his arm.)

…I've got to have some of that food. And he says Duchess, nowhere's going to have black truffles at this time of year. But I said Duke, I had to have it, fly to India for all I care. And then he said I bet if we go backstage, to his dressing room while he's between his turns, that Doctor Faustus could maybe magic you up some. Maybe there's even some left over after the party. He seems like a good man, Duke says, that Wagner seemed to think so, at least, before she left.

(Beat.)

So –

Beat. Bored, FAUSTUS nods to MEPHISTOPHELES who produces a plate of black canapés.

DUCHESS

O my God, I can't believe it, black truffles and –

She eats.

DUCHESS

And Belugian caviar. O my God. Where are they from? They must be from the other side of the world. I told you he would help.

She laughs uproariously and eats one. It's delicious. She eats another.

DUCHESS

Mmm… They're so… They taste so…

She eats with increasing speed. The canapés are never-ending. To DUKE's surprise black saliva starts dribbling from his mouth. He takes out his handkerchief to wipe it away only to find more and more until he is vomiting a stream of black oil into his handkerchief.

FAUSTUS goes to the DUCHESS and kneels before her and listens to her belly.

Shouting is heard off. The SECRET SERVICE MAN and his SWAT TEAM enter in tatters, crutches, wheelchairs and bandages abound.

SECRET SERVICE MAN

There he is. The bastard who did this to us. Go get him men!

Without moving FAUSTUS gestures to MEPHISTOPHELES who, without looking up from her magazine, waves her nail file causing the SECRET SERVICE MAN and the SWAT TEAM to freeze. Enter other characters such as SAXON BRUNO whom FAUSTUS has met on his travels. They shout 'Catch him!', 'Thrush him!', 'Bash him!',

'Burn him!', 'Burst him!', 'Clobber him!', 'Cripple him!', 'Kill him!'.
MEPHISTOPHELES freezes them with a wave of her nail file.

MEPHISTOPHELES
What do you hear?

FAUSTUS
I hear myself as I once was. Innocent.

MEPHISTOPHELES
We all meet ourselves coming home.

FAUSTUS
What is the time?

MEPHISTOPHELES turns up the tannoy, the 'Birdy Song' is playing
out.

STAGE MANAGEMENT
(Over tannoy.)
Dr Faustus and Mephistopheles, one minute to final set of the
night.

She retrieves FAUSTUS' jacket.

MEPHISTOPHELES
Time we went back.

SCENE 18

Enter FAUSTUS' SERVANT.

SERVANT
I think my master means to die shortly,
For he hath given to me all his goods.
And yet methinks if that death were near,
He would not banquet and carouse and swill
Amongst the students, as even now he doth,
Who are at supper with such belly-cheer
As I ne'er beheld in all my life.

Exit SERVANT.

SCENE 19

Enter FAUSTUS with two or three SCHOLARS and
MEPHISTOPHELES.

FIRST SCHOLAR

Master Doctor Faustus, since our conference about fair ladies –
which was the beautifull'st in all the world – we have determined
with ourselves that Helen of Greece was the admirablest lady that
ever lived. Therefore, Master Doctor, if you will do us that favour
as to let us see that peerless dame of Greece, whom all the world
admires for majesty, we should think ourselves much beholding
unto you.

FAUSTUS

Gentlemen, for that I know your friendship is unfeigned, and
Faustus' custom is not to deny the just requests of those that
wish him well, you shall behold that peerless dame of Greece no
otherways for pomp and majesty than when Sir Paris crossed the
seas with her and brought the spoils to rich Dardania. Be silent
then, for danger is in words.

MEPHISTOPHELES goes to the door.

Music sounds. MEPHISTOPHELES returns with HELEN who passes
over the stage.

SECOND SCHOLAR

Too simple is my wit to tell her praise,
Whom all the world admires for majesty.

THIRD SCHOLAR

No marvel though the angry Greeks pursued
With ten years' war the rape of such a queen,
Whose heavenly beauty passeth all compare.

FIRST SCHOLAR

Since we have seen the pride of nature's works
And only paragon of excellence –

Enter WAGNER.

Let us depart; and for this glorious deed
Happy and blest be Faustus evermore.

FAUSTUS

Gentlemen, farewell. The same I wish to you.

Exit SCHOLARS.

WAGNER

O gentle Faustus, leave this damnèd art,
This magic, that will charm thy soul to hell,
And quite bereave thee of salvation – !
Though thou hast now offended like a man,
Do not persever in it like a devil.
Yet, yet thou hast an amiable soul,
If sin by custom grow not into nature;
Then, Faustus, will repentance come too late,
Then thou art banished from the sight of heaven.
No mortal can express the pains of hell.
It may be this my exhortation
Seems harsh, and all unpleasant; let it not,
For, gentle man, I speak it not in wrath,
Or envy of thee, but in tender love,
And pity of thy future misery;
And so have hope that this my kind rebuke,
Checking thy body, may amend thy soul.

FAUSTUS

Where art thou, Faustus? Wretch, what hast thou done?
Damned art thou, Faustus, damned! Despair and die!
Hell calls for right, and with a roaring voice
Says, 'Faustus, come! Thine hour is almost come.'

MEPHISTOPHELES gives him a dagger.

FAUSTUS

And Faustus will come to do thee right.

WAGNER

Oh, stay, good Faustus, stay thy desperate steps!
I see an angel hover o'er thy head,
And with a vial full of precious grace,
Offers to pour the same into thy soul.
Then call for mercy and avoid despair.

FAUSTUS

Ah, my sweet friend, I feel thy words
To comfort my distressèd soul.
Leave me a while to ponder on my sins.

WAGNER

I go, sweet Faustus, but with heavy cheer,
Fearing the ruin of thy hopeless soul.

Exit WAGNER.

FAUSTUS

Accursèd Faustus, where is mercy now?
I do repent, and yet I do despair.
Hell strives with grace for conquest in my breast.
What shall I do to shun the snares of death?

MEPHISTOPHELES

Thou traitor, Faustus, I arrest thy soul
For disobedience to my sovereign lord.
Revolt, or I'll in piecemeal tear thy flesh.

FAUSTUS

I do repent I e'er offended him.
Sweet Mephistopheles, entreat thy lord
To pardon my unjust presumption,
And with my blood again I will confirm
My former vow I made to Lucifer.

MEPHISTOPHELES

Do it then quickly, with unfeignèd heart,
Lest greater dangers do attend thy drift.

FAUSTUS cuts his arm and writes with his blood.

FAUSTUS

Torment, sweet friend, that base and righteous soul
That durst dissuade me from thy Lucifer,
With greatest torments that our hell affords.

MEPHISTOPHELES

Her faith is great. I cannot touch her soul.
But what I may afflict her body with
I will attempt, which is but little worth.

FAUSTUS

One thing, good servant, let me crave of thee
To glut the longing of my heart's desire,
That I might have unto my paramour,
That heavenly Helen which I saw of late,
Whose sweet embracings may extinguish clean
Those thoughts that do dissuade me from my vow,
And keep mine oath I made to Lucifer.

MEPHISTOPHELES

Faustus, this, or what else thou shalt desire,
Shall be performed in twinkling of an eye.

Enter HELEN, brought in by MEPHISTOPHELES.

FAUSTUS

Was this the face that launched a thousand ships
And burnt the topless towers of Ilium?
Sweet Helen, make me immortal with a kiss.

They kiss.

FAUSTUS

Her lips suck forth my soul. See where it flies!
Come, Helen, come, give me my soul again.

They kiss again.

FAUSTUS

Here will I dwell, for heaven is in these lips,
And all is dross that is not Helena!

Enter WAGNER.

FAUSTUS

I will be Paris, and for love of thee
Instead of Troy shall Wittenberg be sacked,
And I will combat with weak Menelaus,
And wear thy colours on my plumèd crest.
Yea, I will wound Achilles in the heel,
And then return to Helen for a kiss.
O, thou art fairer than the evening air,
Clad in the beauty of a thousand stars.
Brighter art thou than flaming Jupiter
When he appeared to hapless Semele,

More lovely than the monarch of the sky
In wanton Arethusa's azure arms;
And none but thou shalt be my paramour.

Exit FAUSTUS and HELEN.

WAGNER

Accursèd Faustus, miserable man,
That from thy soul exclud'st the grace of heaven
And fliest the throne of His tribunal seat!

Enter the DEVILS. They menace WAGNER.

WAGNER

Satan begins to sift me with his pride;
As in this furnace God shall try my faith,
My faith, vile hell, shall triumph over thee.
Ambitious fiends, see how the heavens smile
At your repulse and laughs your state to scorn!
Hence, hell! For hence I fly unto my God.

Exit all in different directions.

SCENE 20

Enter FAUSTUS with the SCHOLARS.

FAUSTUS
Ah, gentlemen!

FIRST SCHOLAR
What ails Faustus?

FAUSTUS
Ah, my sweet chamber-fellow! Had I lived with thee, then had I lived still, but now I die eternally. Look, comes he not? Comes he not?

SECOND SCHOLAR
What means Faustus?

THIRD SCHOLAR
Belike he is grown into some sickness by being over-solitary.

FIRST SCHOLAR
If it be so, we'll have physicians to cure him.
(To FAUSTUS.)
'Tis but a surfeit. Never fear, man.

FAUSTUS
A surfeit of deadly sin that hath damned both body and soul.

SECOND SCHOLAR
Yet, Faustus, look up to heaven. Remember God's mercies are infinite.

FAUSTUS
But Faustus' offence can ne'er be pardoned. The serpent that tempted Eve may be saved, but not Faustus. Ah, gentlemen, hear me with patience, and tremble not at my speeches. Though my heart pants and quivers to remember that I have been a student here these thirty years, O, would I had never seen Wittenberg, never read book! And what wonders I have done, all Germany can witness, yea, all the world, for which Faustus hath lost both Germany and the world, yea, heaven itself – heaven, the seat of God, the throne of the blessed, the kingdom of joy – and must remain in hell for ever. Hell, ah, hell, for ever! Sweet friends, what shall become of Faustus, being in hell forever?

THIRD SCHOLAR
Yet, Faustus, call on God.

FAUSTUS
On God, whom Faustus hath abjured? On God, whom Faustus
hath blasphemed? Ah, my God, I would weep, but the devil
draws in my tears. Gush forth blood instead of tears, yea, life and
soul. O, he stays my tongue! I would lift up my hands, but see,
they hold them, they hold them.

ALL
Who, Faustus?

FAUSTUS
Lucifer and Mephistopheles. Ah, gentlemen! I gave them my soul
for my cunning.

ALL
God forbid!

FAUSTUS
God forbade it indeed, but Faustus hath done it. For vain pleasure
of four-and-twenty years hath Faustus lost eternal joy and felicity.
I writ them a bill with mine own blood. The date is expired, the
time will come, and he will fetch me.

FIRST SCHOLAR
Why did not Faustus tell us of this before?

FAUSTUS
Oft have I thought to have done so, but the devil threatened to
tear me in pieces if I named God, to fetch both body and soul if I
once gave ear to divinity. And now 'tis too late. Gentlemen, away,
lest you perish with me.

SECOND SCHOLAR
O, what shall we do to save Faustus?

FAUSTUS
Talk not of me, but save yourselves and depart.

THIRD SCHOLAR
I will stay with Faustus.

FIRST SCHOLAR

(To the THIRD SCHOLAR.)

Let us into the next room.

FAUSTUS

Ay, pray for me, pray for me! And what noise soever ye hear, come not unto me, for nothing can rescue me.

SECOND SCHOLAR

Pray thou, and we will pray that God may have mercy upon thee.

FAUSTUS

Gentlemen, farewell. If I live till morning, I'll visit you; if not, Faustus is gone to hell.

ALL

Faustus, farewell.

Exit SCHOLARS.

The clock strikes eleven.

FAUSTUS

Ah, Faustus,
Now hast thou but one bare hour to live,
And then thou must be damned perpetually.
Stand still, you ever-moving spheres of heaven,
That time may cease and midnight never come!
Fair nature's eye, rise, rise again, and make
Perpetual day; or let this hour be but
A year, a month, a week, a natural day,
That Faustus may repent and save his soul!
O lente, lente currite noctis equi!
The stars move still; time runs; the clock will strike;
The devil will come, and Faustus must be damned.
O, I'll leap up to my God! Who pulls me down?
See, see, where Christ's blood streams in the firmament!
One drop would save my soul, half a drop. Ah, my Christ!
Ah, rend not my heart for naming of my Christ!
Yet will I call on him. O, spare me, Lucifer!
Where is it now? 'Tis gone; and see where God
Stretcheth out his arm and bends his ireful brows!
Mountains and hills, come, come and fall on me,

And hide me from the heavy wrath of God!
No, no!
Then will I headlong run into the earth.
Earth, gape! O, no, it will not harbour me.
You stars that reigned at my nativity,
Whose influence hath allotted death and hell,
Now draw up Faustus like a foggy mist
Into the entrails of yon labouring cloud,
That when you vomit forth into the air,
My limbs may issue from your smoky mouths,
So that my soul may but ascend to heaven.

The clock strikes the half-hour.

FAUSTUS
Ah, half the hour is past!
'Twill all be past anon.
O God, if thou wilt not have mercy on my soul,
Yet for Christ's sake, whose blood hath ransomed me,
Impose some end to my incessant pain.
Let Faustus live in hell a thousand years,
A hundred thousand, and at last be saved.
O, no end is limited to damnèd souls.
Why wert thou not a creature wanting soul?
Or why is this immortal that thou hast?
Ah, Pythagoras' metempsychosis, were that true,
This soul should fly from me and I be changed
Unto some brutish beast.
All beasts are happy, for, when they die,
Their souls are soon dissolved in elements;
But mine must live still to be plagued in hell.
Curst be the parents that engendered me!
No, Faustus, curse thyself, curse Lucifer,
That hath deprived thee of the joys of heaven.

The clock strikes twelve.

FAUSTUS
O, it strikes, it strikes! Now, body, turn to air,
Or Lucifer will bear thee quick to hell.

Thunder and lightning.

FAUSTUS

O soul, be changed into little waterdrops,
And fall into the ocean, ne'er be found!
My God, my god, look not so fierce on me!

Enter LUCIFER, MEPHISTOPHELES and other DEVILS.

FAUSTUS

Adders and serpents, let me breathe a while!
Ugly hell, gape not. Come not, Lucifer!
I'll burn my books: Ah, Mephistopheles!

Exit DEVILS with FAUSTUS.

SCENE 21

Enter CHORUS.

CHORUS
Cut is the branch that might have grown full straight,
And burnèd is Apollo's laurel bough,
That sometime grew within this learnèd man.
Faustus is gone. Regard his hellish fall,
Whose fiendful fortune may exhort the wise
Only to wonder at unlawful things,
Whose deepness doth entice such forward wits
To practice more than heavenly power permits.

Exit all.